"Every day women contact me because they know things are very wrong in their relationship but they can't manage to walk away. Usually they tell me, "I love him so much," and that can be after he's thrown them down the stairs and broken their arm. All too often I am pleading with them to leave before they're killed.

But domestic abuse isn't only about violence. These days we have better understanding of coercive control – the sort of abusive behaviour that doesn't necessarily involve physical violence but utterly undermines self-worth and autonomy.

Many have family and friends who love them but in their frustration say things like, "I'm going to have nothing more to do with you unless you leave him." The trouble is this leaves someone vulnerable even more isolated and at risk.

This moving collection of searing personal accounts from the inside of abusive relationships helps those of us who haven't directly experienced this ourselves understand what a honey trap abusers can set, how gradual the progression and gaslighting, how utterly demoralizing the end game. But for the grace … In identifying with these women's experiences we also come to understand how best to support anyone in our own lives we may be worried about.

And for those who fall on these accounts with recognition and light dawning because they are so like their own story, there will be the relief of knowing you are not alone and vital clues to the route to freedom."

- Deidre Sanders, *This Morning* agony aunt

D0543588

"Domestic abuse is a serious blight on our society. Last year almost 60,000 instances were reported to police authorities. Who can doubt that sad figure, horrific in itself, is only confirmation of a much greater level of unreported individual suffering for those who have to endure physical and psychological violence by partners within their own homes.

This powerful book lays the problem bare in brutally frank and harrowing terms through the personal stories of a number of women who have endured abuse, sometimes for many years on end. They reveal the terrible human realities which lie behind the published statistics.

There is, however, light as well as darkness in these pages as the women recount how, with determination and courage, they finally managed to escape the clutches of those who had made their lives a misery and went on to live happier and more fulfilling lives as a result.

All associated with this project deserve the highest praise for bringing these individual histories into the public domain.

The book merits the widest possible readership in today's Scotland."

- Sir Tom Devine, Historian and Author

"This book is important because it is the truth of domestic abuse, told by the women who have lived it.

Domestic abuse is ugly and cruel but the women have imbued their stories with a beauty of language, with heart and with hope.

To read it, is to travel with these survivors on an emotional and painful journey but also to arrive with them, to a place of empowerment, where in the pages of this book, their voices are suppressed no longer."

- Annie Brown, *Daily Record*

"A soul-baring and inspirational read from survivors of domestic violence who have overcome common themes of power, control and domination to live independently without fear of abuse, neglect and harm: A must read for men and women!

- Michael Alexander, *The Courier*

Her-story Rewritten

True stories of women and girls surviving partner abuse

Compiled by
Saje Scotland

Editor Nadia Karim

Cover Illustration by Gwen Gemmell

ISBN: 978-0-244-82473-0

PublishNation
www.publishnation.co.uk

CONTENTS

Dedication   ix

Foreword by Janet of Saje Scotland   xi

On the Road Called Freedom   1

Smile   3

Time   17

Soaring   19

This Is Me   47

Fighting Against the Desolation of Me   54

Household Bast*rd   64

Daring   66

Unstoppable   79

Staying Alive   86

Never Give Up   91

Being A Parent   92

Peace   95

Blue   104

Shattered Dreams   107

Feeling Brand New Without You   123

Thoughts   124

Jigsaw   125

Hidden   138

It's Okay Not To Be Okay   142

The Love I Deserved   151

Power   153

#Freedom   158

The Spaces In Between   160

Love?   192

My Story   195

Extracts From My Diary   200

Reflection   204

Acknowledgements   217

Find Help   218

Follow Our Campaign   219

DEDICATION

This book is a tribute to every single woman and girl who is living with or has lived through partner abuse.

The stories and poems are written by women who have made their way to Saje Scotland, a small charity supporting women and children who have lived in controlling and harmful relationships.

These women have come through the other side. Through support, love and sheer inner strength, they have found the incredible courage not only to write down their truth but to share it with strangers. This book would not exist without them. Although each story is unique, the book is full of shared experience. It is the same old story, acted out in nuanced ways: the story of control. It is their stories written in their own words. The hope is that those who read it will first believe and finally know that life can change.

This book is a chronicle of domestic abuse in all its guises. Domestic abuse can happen to anyone. It cuts right across the globe, across our ideas of class, race and religion, across what we think it means to be strong or weak, young or old.

It arose directly out of the work we do with women, and, though inclusion is at the heart of every project we undertake, the book's content stemmed from those women who chose to share their stories; who, ultimately, were all women abused by their male partners. We reached out to all our service users to participate in this book, but many were not yet able or willing to share their stories, and this book does not represent the diversity of experience in regard to sexuality that we see in our grassroots work. We fully recognise that domestic abuse happens in same-sex relationships, and we fully acknowledge that men can have similar experiences within their relationships, too. We hope this book opens up a wider conversation that resonates with and reflects all people.

This book goes beyond platitudes and pleasantries, and the language reflects that. Some women chose to censor their swearing; others use graphic language. From the outset, we all fiercely agreed that each contributor must have the right to tell her story however she'd like to, in her most authentic voice.

This book does not make for easy reading but, like any space set aside for women to share their collective stories, it is also full of moments of humour, joy and hope. Sitting together around a table at the first planning meeting for this book, when the women were still uncertain about how to even begin to write about their experiences, the overriding sense in the room was that this must be a book that explains why it is so difficult to leave an abusive relationship. We hope it explains why leaving isn't as easy as just packing a bag and walking out the door. Why it takes many women dozens of attempts before they leave. The second consensus was that it must be a book that shows how much joy in life can be found on the other side of that door.

FOREWORD

by Janet Henderson,
Saje Scotland

The business bit

All profits from this book go directly to Saje Scotland to finance the charity and continue the work we do.

The birth, life and times
of Saje Scotland

Why did it all start?

Domestic abuse is a term commonly used. However, it has different meanings to different individuals. Many women do not think their relationship is abusive. They know there is something wrong; they know they are being controlled, harmed emotionally, victimised, manipulated, coerced, sexually abused, intimidated, worn down, blamed, humiliated, mocked, and disrespected. Some believe it must incorporate physical violence for it to be deemed abuse. To cover the immeasurable range of violence, coercion and harm we will use two small words, *domestic abuse*.

A life feeling worthless and abused becomes normalised.

And yet, domestic abuse is still so hidden. It's shrouded in secrecy and there is still a culture of blame towards those who live with domestic abuse. Questions and statements such as, *'Why didn't she just leave if it was that bad?'*, *'Why did she go back?'* or *'I wouldn't put up with that,'* are alarmingly common.

Women are silenced by the judgement of others, by the shame and fear, and wrongly-held feelings of blame.

No one thinks they are going to find themselves in an abusive relationship. No one tells women or girls what behaviours to look out for or that certain behaviour in a relationship is abusive. No one really discusses how hard it is to leave an abusive relationship nor the devastating, long term impact that abuse can have on women and their children.

Where can women voice to others extremely personal, traumatic abuse without fear of being judged, ashamed and embarrassed, or thought of as stupid or weak?

The beginnings of Saje Scotland

Saje Scotland would not exist were it not for my good friend, Sally Sinclair, her passion and her drive. Her chivvying, motivation, and deep belief in supporting women and girls drove us on. Thank you, Sally Sinclair.

In March 2012, our separate work contracts ended simultaneously, and it was then we thought *let's start the organisation now*. We opened Saje Scotland.

Sally sadly got quite ill and consequently decided to retire. I still miss her in the workplace today, but thankfully she made a full recovery. We are still besties and continue to put the world to rights many an evening over a bottle of wine or three.

From our small beginnings we have grown to become a respected, valued charity.

What We Do

Saje gives women the space and openness they need to feel in order to share their experiences:

'As soon as I got married my husband insisted on being in the bathroom with me. Showers or baths, he was there sitting on the loo 'chatting'. When I found the courage to say this out loud at group, I was completely blown away with the responses. Other women nodded and spoke about similar intrusive experiences and the feelings they had at the time and still carry. We had a frank and honest discussion. The shame I had carried round for ages was put into perspective and I stopped feeling like a 'freak and batshit crazy'. Listening to others' feelings was the singularly most impactful moment of my life. I can barely express the sense of relief and freedom at that session. I feel so proud I took that leap and told my story. It enabled others to talk of their 'shame' and as the weeks progressed, we could talk about our most horrendous experiences in a safe and supported environment'. (P)

Saje Scotland has evolved into a holistic organisation. We have developed a variety of programmes looking at the massive range of abusive behaviour and the horrendous impacts on lives: courses that build assertiveness, confidence, esteem and resetting personal boundaries, alongside inspiration and motivation courses. Additionally, developed as a result of feedback on what is needed from women and organisations, we designed specialised programmes for women with learning disabilities, lesbian and bi-sexual women, women in the criminal justice system, and women with substance misuse issues.

We also deliver the amazing Freedom Programme. Widely accessible across the UK, the Freedom Programme and 'Living with the Dominator' book is the intellectual property of Pat Craven.

You can find out more at: www.freedomprogramme.co.uk.

We are proud to also be delivering a Young People programme in schools.

And we have a course for professionals based on what women want professionals to know about the complexities of abuse.

To support women in their journey of change, community education workers, adult basic education workers and employment workers come into groups, offering participants a range of options.

We have *Drop in Cafes* which serve as a place for women to keep connected and for potential participants to come to chat. Often, other services attend to chat about what they can offer.

We can only provide the range of work mentioned above because of volunteers. Every volunteer we work alongside has completed our programmes and been trained to deliver services to their peer group. It works.

And, of course, this incredible book would not have happened without the amazing and strong women who have completed these courses, and their courage to write their stories.

Why We Compiled This Book
The stories you are about to read all incorporate a range of abusive behaviours. There is a thread of similarity through them all, yet at the same time all are so very, very different.

This book offers a message of empathy. Through the stories, indicators of domestic abuse, which often go unnoticed, may be seen and understood. Hopefully, anyone reading the book will better understand the complexities of how and why someone experiencing abuse might try their hardest to keep up appearances and minimise the abuse. Hopefully, you will be more able to read between the lines and ask the right questions. By being the worker who believes. By being the friend who offers a safe place to stay. The neighbour who doesn't just walk on by. By not allowing men who do choose to perpetuate abuse against women to hide behind the "norms" of machoism. By bringing the fear, shame and violence into the light. By teaching our sons the strength in true equality. And teaching our daughters the strength in sisterhood.

ON THE ROAD
CALLED FREEDOM

To understand what it is like
to live your life with a monster.
Forget everything you ever imagined
and let me take you along my journey.

You're on the edge of a dangerous cliff which is crumbling at each
movement of your feet
across on the other side is everyone you love so dear,
they are slowly fading into the dark and away from your heart and
soul
and your cries and screams are silent.

The space between you gets bigger and bigger
and you can't reach out or move
as you're getting held tighter and tighter
by the monster who is smiling behind you.

He lets you watch them from the cliff
as he likes to give you hope each day,
but one false move he has not authorised
and he tells you that you won't see them again.

Day after day, night after night
the days go by so slow but fast,
His grip gets tighter every time
it never is his last.

Battered and bruised inside and out
tired and confused with all the games,
you give in and fully submit,
this is just how it's going to be.

When the monster senses your submission
he releases your chains as he knows,
but then the clouds part and the suns sends a ray,
a tiny glimmer of hope shines through.

The you that once was becomes louder and clearer
shouting at us to survive.
That voice from within claims our freedom once more
the one that the monster thought he had buried.

Then out from the ashes we rise once again
this time we smash through the chains.
We spent so much time watching him play
we can now play him at his own game.

Through wisdom, fear, bravery and hope
we take back our freedom once more
we have defeated the monster and left him wounded
and get up on our feet and run free.

We are now on the road called FREEDOM
and have all we once had and more.
We now have strength, liberation and love,
United we are prisoners no more!

SMILE

We met when I was 18 and he was 23, through our social circles and we were nothing more than acquaintances for the first year. He was engaged and living with someone else. I was single and naïve about relationships and guys, with the innocence of growing up in a small town with a relatively drama free family and a good group of friends. I was working in an office full-time. I liked going to the gym a couple of times a week, spending time with family and going out with my friends at the weekends. I was quiet, hardworking...probably seemed a little serious. I had a dry sense of humour and got on well with everyone – always had a smile. I was shy around men, though I didn't really know why. I lived with my Dad and had a good relationship with him, with my brother and with other male relatives and friends – all of whom were decent and trustworthy. I had a few boyfriends but none lasted longer than a few weeks and I didn't really know why – I just expected to meet someone I got on with and they'd like me enough to stick around.

I'm 38 now and we're divorced. We've been apart for 3 years. When my ex-husband and I started our relationship...as we built our life together; went through uni together; got fulfilling, rewarding jobs; bought a house; got married; had our daughter and two years later, our son; the one big thing that I was absolutely, determinedly and passionately not going to do was be divorced. That was not going to happen to me and my family like it had to us when I was in my teens. We talked – my ex-husband and I – we argued and we talked about how much we loved each other and how much we wanted each other to be happy and wanted our children to be happy and about how happy we were together, all of us and the talking (some shouting) and all of the words were right and they drowned out the facts that

3

what was happening in our relationship was the complete, exact, total opposite of love and happiness.

It is so hard to put into words all of the hundreds and thousands of apparently small, insignificant, easily forgivable ways that he managed to have my every thought and action geared towards meeting his needs…and it feels impossible for me to explain how I couldn't see that's what was happening – how I was so well conditioned to maximizing his wants and needs and minimising, suppressing, not even noticing that I had my own and they should have been holding equal importance and consideration.

When he asked me out, a year after we first met – this good looking, fun, charming, friendly, popular, down-to-earth and now single guy – I didn't hesitate. I was delighted! He put me at ease and made me feel comfortable, attractive and wanted. All I'd ever wanted was someone to love, who loved me, wanted the same things I did…there he was! Were there warning signs? Oh my God, Yes! There were hundreds from the very beginning which the beauty of hindsight allows me to see with crystal clarity. Not at the time though. At the time, I felt sorry for him when he told me his ex-fiancée had hit him – unprovoked. A few years later, once I had hurt him physically – very much provoked – literally pushed up against the wall in our hall, the front door locked and the key in his pocket - scared and overwhelmed and vulnerable – desperate for space from this heated argument, space that he decided I wasn't allowed…by then I could picture a different scene: him and the ex who hit him…but it was too late for me by then. It was a warning sign I didn't see when we got engaged after 4 months. I was just flattered and happy – giddy…at 20, in no hurry to get married, but delighted someone wanted to marry me and build a life together. He wanted to have children and he idolized his parent's happy marriage. I just felt so lucky.

There were always stories of incidents he was unhappy with – he'd come to me and say people were talking – usually rumours of him and another girl. He flirted with everyone he met. I felt secure in our relationship – he appeared to adore me, and I didn't get jealous – or maybe I didn't want to appear jealous. So these stories were marked with his dissatisfaction at how *unfair it was, folk always talking about him when he'd not done anything, would never do anything*...and I would believe him - he was very upset – I would comfort him and reassure him that of course I trusted him, I wasn't going to listen to idle gossip over him...I loved him and love means trust.

In the 6 years between us becoming a couple and getting married, I thought I was happy. Looking back, I think actually my expectations of what a relationship should be like and how a partner should behave were just pretty low. We spent the first four years basically long distance, as each of us moved up and down the country for university. He had an unskilled labouring job when we met, but I could tell he was intelligent. I encouraged him to pursue a qualification in a subject he was passionate about, then I followed him and found a course in the same area – 300 miles away from home and everything I knew. I loved him and love means support, encouragement to follow dreams. For one of those years we did live in the same house. The rest of the time, there was some distance – even when sharing a house with another flatmate, I was happier having my own bedroom. I pushed down my niggling doubts that this maybe wasn't how things were supposed to be. Maybe sometimes, friends, family, people we met, might show surprise that we were engaged but living separately, despite having moved all that way from home. I reasoned that we needed space to study. We spoke every single day at the same time – that's devotion! And we told each other how much we loved each other and I thought that this was just us putting the groundwork in for our life together and then, once that's done, it'll be better and we can be together like a proper couple. If ever I asked for anything of him, whatever I felt...his need and feelings were bigger, stronger, more urgent, held higher importance. I felt at the time if we talked, that I'd been heard and understood. I couldn't argue with the words – the words were always right for the situation...but somehow I'd find myself comforting him, resolving to give him more, or just...be different and better. I felt sorry for him. As he had begun to trust me more and more, he had shared very personal and distressing experiences he'd suffered as a child. Abused by a close family member. Neglect, really, by those who should have protected him. And I was alarmed and I did worry that he was only telling me and that people often need solid, professional support to deal with these things and that without it, patterns have a habit of repeating...but no, it was only for me to carry...you see, he could *only trust me and he didn't need to think about that, it was too upsetting and distressing* and I loved him and love means respect, doesn't it – so...Yes, he just needed more love and more support. I just needed to love him more and support him more and comfort him and that would make everything OK.

We had an extremely difficult time when our first child was tiny and I spoke to our Health Visitor because I knew he needed help. Social Services became involved – they had reason to worry about the baby's safety. Once again, his need was greater – *he felt so bad, so low, so out of his depth, so frustrated with himself...* and I just needed to do more, be more, then it would be OK. Because I married him in sickness and in health; for better and for worse...we dreamed of this for so long and when one of you is weak, the other one just needs to step up, don't they – that is love and I loved him and I loved her and I loved our family and I just needed to make it all OK. And I think the most confusing thing of all is that it's not him telling me this – I think all this for myself and it's my choice to stay and fight and love and just keep going – because he needs us, doesn't he...he would be lost without us – have nothing to live for – who could do that to someone they love? And I do remember feeling that others wondered why I made that choice and they seemed to not agree. And I did feel like every day was a struggle and there was a dark, heavy blanket over me that I couldn't shift and this wasn't how it was meant to be but I am strong and I can get through this…nothing lasts forever and it will get better – I just need to keep going…for all of us. The next few years are a haze of nappies and milestones, feeding, weaning, toilet training, toddler groups, housework, part-time paid work…the familiar juggle of family life. Our son arrived when our daughter was two…I felt driven to grow our family and create a fresh start: proving my love and trust for him and faith in us and we wanted more than one child. In hindsight, the difficulties he had experienced on becoming a Father should have led any reasonable woman to at least wait much longer. Denial ran through my core I think…we continuously sold ourselves this story of a loving, happy couple and a happy, healthy family and other people certainly seemed to believe it so it must be true. I didn't know of hyper-vigilance until my Women's Aid worker used this word in the months following our split. This was just my permanent state – did every working mum not just have to be very organised and always busy, running right on time or slightly late, irritated by unexpected little blips of life that needed attended to on top of everything I already had to do every day. I couldn't even guess at which point I lost myself because I don't think I knew myself very well to start with. I just thought this was life – you grow up, get a job, marry, have a family, see your loved ones and keep everything ticking over – make sure everyone is happy all the time so that it all looks OK and this is it. He worked, full-time – in a job he loved, but didn't pay very well, but it made him happy so that was good. To start with, I worked in a job which paid well but was very hard and not enjoyable, then I found something that made me happy but didn't pay well and I carried the responsibility of budgeting for our household, with an income that was never really enough. And when *he'd look sad and guilty for wanting something that we couldn't really afford and I'd listen to him explain how he works hard and wished he earned more and he'd just like to be able to treat himself now and again but it's not fair because I can't treat myself either and* I'd smile and find myself pulling together enough for what he wanted as we slipped into debt for the last week of the month's food, or when the car needed fixed, or Christmas comes…because he works hard and he deserves it.

If this doesn't sound like abuse…because I don't think mine is your average story so maybe it doesn't, but having lived it for 16 years – although I know it was – I also still minimize his behaviour and excuse it and try to be balanced and fair and suppress the feelings – I mean stuff them right, really far down, because to feel them would just be too much…If it doesn't feel like abuse, let me explain that eventually I gave up trying to discuss things with him. If I wasn't happy…if I felt like maybe I needed help, or needed to talk, maybe there was something he might do differently to help…I always picked the wrong time to raise it. *He was tired, from all his hard work; we'd had a nice day, why spoil it; he just started watching this programme…it was just always a bad time and I was overreacting and making him frustrated and then what about those times when I did x, y, z and he was upset* – even though they didn't seem to relate at all to what I'd wanted to talk about…I'm so confused and I'd try to get back to my point and *if I cried I was trying to make him feel bad and if I stayed cool and calm when he got angry and shouted well that was because I was cold* and when I stopped arguing because there was no point – it just fueled his anger which scared me and I wasn't being heard anyway, but I wasn't allowed to end the argument, because he still had stuff to say and I wasn't allowed space – he'd follow me to the bathroom and stand outside banging on the door and shouting at me, trying to unlock the door from the outside – it wasn't done 'til he was done. Once he squeezed my arm and left finger shaped bruises and the next day when I pointed them out, he looked disgusted and said "Who did that? It wasn't me" as if

I must have bruised myself to make it look worse than it was. Even just that dismissive, unbelieving tone made me doubt myself. I felt angry – I shouldn't have bruises on me because of his aggression – it did strike me more that I could see evidence the next day. *But...he doesn't believe it was him? He didn't mean to hold so hard, then...just a bit carried away in the heat of the moment.* He'd gotten angrier because I'd gone to the bathroom and locked the door – if I'd just been a bit stronger and been able to stay and talk it out, that probably wouldn't have happened. I obviously can't tell anyone about this – that he hurt me – because that's abuse, isn't it, and everyone would tell me to leave. But it's not like he punches me – he's never punched me – or kicked me or made me bleed. And, actually, I hurt him first didn't I – all those years ago though he still remembers and still reminds me. In his condescending, patronizing sneer *I hurt him first* – yes, that's why we fight like this now. And it's not like it's physical very often. I don't want anyone to get the wrong idea because most of our days are OK; we get along, we laugh, we love each other. We say it every day, so that's definitely true. We bicker, of course, and we don't always agree but that's just because we've been together so long isn't it. It's just what life is like: tired, kids, health, family, work, finances...'til death do us part. The other times he's hurt me, when it's got out of hand...he is so upset with himself after; *he knows he's gone too far and he knows I should leave and he is so, so, sorry. He's prepared to do whatever it takes to make amends and he's so, so scared of losing everything we have together,* everything we've worked so hard for – our house, our garden, our family, our lives, wider family and friends. It's all ours together and I love him and I can't imagine my life without him... our life without him... just can't be.

And it does continue, it does get worse, somehow, though I can't say how or why or when... temporarily better with guilt and promises, then worse but it's hazy. It isn't horrific every day though and friends and family are there and nobody sees. And I feel relief when other people are there because he is full of compliments and fun and kindness and charm…they are envious, they say so…it must be a laugh a minute in your house! At first I say nothing and then it starts to irritate me because it's so far from the truth…I dryly suggest that it's not quite like that but they don't hear what I mean because he's a great guy and nobody's perfect, obviously he'll have the occasional off day, but he's such a great guy. The children look healthy and do well at nursery and school and sometimes I see them scared when he shouts, or looks a certain way – he intimidates them and I know it and if I'm very careful with my wording and tone and I get the timing exactly right, I can manage it and keep things OK and I'll take over and see to them. *Why don't you sit there, you'll be tired after your day* - it's OK, I'll see to what needs done. We are always very quiet in the morning, because he needs quiet, he is tired and I dread if the children can't sleep or are ill because if he wakes up he's in a mood and it's best if we try to get everything right, the way he's happiest, otherwise there's upset and stress and it's just exhausting and…it's just best to avoid that, however we can.

It does start to gradually seep into my awareness that I am starting to label some things "unacceptable," yet I continue to accept them. But when I try to talk to him, I get the time wrong. He reminds me of "unacceptable" things I've done too, which obviously cancel out his unacceptable behaviour. Stupid me! I do start to realise, these things are not going to change. He has promised change, but it does not change. And he points out – when things get so heated that I say I think we can't go on like this, we need some time apart – that he works full time and pays the bills, so if I want us to separate, I would have to leave. The children and I would have to leave our home. I would have to take the children and stay somewhere else. But where would I stay? Because I am ashamed and embarrassed to not be able to sort out my difficulties with my husband between ourselves, in our own home. And we have already tried counselling and so we have *done that* and it obviously *didn't work* and obviously *he tried his best and it's down to me – I am controlling, he tells me and I just need to relax more – I'm too uptight.* So, I have family who have space for us and I know we could stay with, but they live too far away to manage school and nursery and I work from home and couldn't do that there so I couldn't get it to work and I know anyway, I love him, and it would only be a temporary split because we do want to be together and so why would I put us all through that? And things like this don't happen to people like me, or people like us don't do things like this – it just all feels like too much drama and everyone would be upset and my family would be alarmed and upset if they found out that these things are happening and they didn't know.

Then at some point I had a friend who'd separated from her husband and our situations seemed similar – he was the breadwinner, but she stayed in the house with the kids and he moved out. And then I was clearer and stronger – that is the right thing, for the children to remain with the familiarity of their home. And the right thing for the children, well that's the right thing! So, he is just wrong, actually, and if that was to happen to us – it's not, but if it was – it would be him who should leave, not me.

Once, I managed to tell that friend that the night before I'd left in the car to get some space as things had blown up. It had been bath time, so the children were there and awake and the only thing I could do to stop the argument in front of them was leave the house. She said exactly what I needed her to say, which was: *if you ever need somewhere to go, you can always come to mine, no questions asked. There is always space for you and the children here.* The next time I needed to leave, I knew she was out, so I didn't go, but afterwards I told another friend of the offer and she said the same. Knowing I had two places I could turn up with no warning, not needing to give an explanation, that was probably the most valuable thing I could have right then. To not cause more drama, or have to face my family knowing and judging him for it, because I still love him, remember, and I want us to be together because I can't imagine anything else and he loves me and he's the father of my children, so I don't want my family doubting him and judging us. I had no idea then but these conversations and the kindness and pure acceptance from my friends – this was a game changer. It gave me the validation I needed – it actually is OK to need to be somewhere else and to not have to explain? Wow, I totally did not know that.

The next step came completely out of the blue and was the beginning of the end. I got a message from an old friend – an ex-colleague – congratulating me on my tenth wedding anniversary. He was envious that we were still together and happy after all this time. He compared that to his own shorter relationships over the same length of time and I was quick to reply, "Facebook doesn't show the full story." Like a thread begging to be pulled at, I liked his openness and honesty; his genuine interest and frank way of broaching this real-life stuff. It was just that everything aligned. The right combination at the right time.

I had posted pictures of our anniversary night away. We looked solid and normal and happy. I let my story unravel to my friend and it started with me believing my marriage was strong, but not perfect...we have hard times, but we work together and keep going, talking, listening, helping. I found myself giving him relationship advice and opening up about what had happened when my daughter was a baby. He listened and encouraged me to talk and he was interested. He was respectful and kind and he never questioned anything I said other than to ascertain facts – it surprised me not to feel judged and doubted. After a couple of days or so, I realised I was detailing the history of my husband's violence towards me and how I'd managed to get a step further ahead each time. From the first time when he'd had the house locked and the key in his pocket – no escape. Next time I had the key, so I'd got out, but could only walk and he might come out looking for me...couldn't go far, so didn't feel safe – obviously my leaving will have angered him more than when we were fighting in the house. A time after that I'd had the car keys, but nowhere to go. I found myself explaining that now I have friends who know and will give me somewhere to go so...wait. Why the FUCK am I waiting for this to happen again? Hit me like a bolt, seeing it written like that – words on the screen and hearing the description of progressive steps in my head. This is obviously going to happen again. I shouldn't be waiting for it to happen again.

Within a week, I realised that the way I felt now – having someone to listen to me without judging, encouraging me, honouring my feelings, just be there while I figured myself out – that's how I really should be feeling in my marriage, not with someone else. I connected with myself in a way that I hadn't known was possible, let alone realised I was missing and I just knew something huge was happening...knew I could trust it was for the best and I just had to go with it. All those times I had thought quietly to myself "One day, you'll push me too far" and without any big dramatic incident, they had culminated at the right time – this was the time to end it. I went very focused and instinctive – deciding when I needed it done and how. I needed my Dad there to make sure he'd leave – I knew I couldn't do that on my own – he'd cry and beg and promise and say he had nowhere to go. He did all that but it didn't have the same effect it had before, with the support there for me to follow through.

I knew it was over before I knew it was abuse. A good friend with professional experience in the subject used the word and I knew she wouldn't use it lightly. I might still not know that that's what it was, if she hadn't have said. I know that might sound ridiculous, but I knew nothing of boundaries when it came to emotional well-being.

The physical stuff I knew was wrong, but there was always an explanation that I had provoked it and each time felt few and far between. I was confused and felt responsible...all the time, for everything. Recognising that his behaviour towards me was abusive opened a door to a great deal of support – from Saje and their courses, Women's Aid, CEDAR, with housing – even setting up formal maintenance payments from him for the children. I saw myself as capable, but I did need all the help I could get with this. Taking the time to understand the complexity of abuse, to heal and learn about healthy behaviour and change my expectations, has enabled me to make my life and my children's lives unrecognisable from that time.

The day after he left – I felt euphoric. That feeling continued for weeks, and even lasted through having to communicate with him about money, the children, our house; while he continued to try to get inside my head. There was an instant sense of peace in the house. The children felt it too, though they were upset, aged 8 and 6 to not have Dad there. We could start to relax now – no-one's temper to tiptoe around. For the first time ever, it was safe to show if we felt anything other than happy and excited. It just wasn't OK before to be sad, or angry, confused, disappointed. We were free to be ourselves now. With support and encouragement and the experience of people who "got it" – I learnt how to calmly and assertively stick to my point when he tried his tactics, attempting to bend me to his will. I got an additional phone, just for essential communication with him, so I could stop feeling anxious every time it beeped and get some headspace to help focus on my own thoughts and feelings, rather than grasping to fight what I knew he was thinking. I still hear his voice now, sneering at me and telling anyone who'll listen that *he's the victim, I am controlling and unreasonable – I abused him....that I want to keep our kids away from him...he's trying his best but I am never happy.* I had to work hard but it is much easier now to remind myself of the facts and separate it from his power hungry, warped view.

We had two years just the three of us and I'm proud of myself for that and pleased with how we spent that time. I believe it was one of the best things I could have done for us – staying single and focusing on our new life as a family of three. I could have stayed single for longer – maybe forever – such was the paralysing fear at the thought of even talking to a man, much less venturing into any kind of relationship. A year ago, I met a man who I felt instantly was different. He radiated respect and kindness. As we got to know each other, I examined for warning signs thoroughly, everywhere and I found, consistently: openness, honest, straightforward communication, fun, patience…more kindness and respect and affection without agenda.

I was happy before but what I had to do to achieve that feeling took tremendous effort every day and a great denial of parts of myself and of the reality around me. I am happy now without such effort, just because life is good. I have good, solid, trustworthy people around me who genuinely want the best for us and will go out of their way to help. I have time – way more time than before, because the freedom to decide how I spend it is mine. I have a safe home – properly safe and full of fun. I used to smile because it made me feel happier; now, I feel happy and that makes me smile.

HOPE

TIME

Time is an illusion
A mass of great delusion
Filled with much confusion

What has been
What has gone
What is now
When is now

Everything is now
How?

The past is not the past
The future has not been cast
The present has no mast
The devastation is vast

Memories have no place in time
Memories have no place to shine
Memories are now
How?

Apprehension, trepidation, agitation
No time at all for meditation

Flashbacks darting here and there
Nowhere safe, not here, not there

Double life's
Double images
Double visions
Double troubles

Stuck within the loop of time
Stuck within the fragile mind
Stuck in moments filled with fear
Stuck with nothing to hold dear

Timelines merging into one
You cannot run into the sun
Timelines shooting into pain
However will I live again

Self sabotage
Self-destruct
Self harm
The power of the mind and time combined

Time can steal
Time can heal
The moments in time that are raw and real

Time is an illusion
Whilst Stuck in deep dark confusion

SOARING

"Why didn't you just leave?"
"Why did you put up with that?"
"Are you stupid, get out now!"
"I would never tolerate that!"
"I would never let that happen to me!"

Those are just a few of the comments and statements that you are
met with when you dare to mention that age old taboo subject -
domestic abuse.

Straight away you are bombarded with an array of hard-hitting
opinions from the person you have finally built up the courage to
confide in. Initially you are shot down in flames. You are consumed
and overcome with guilt, fear and shame. Left wishing you had just
kept your mouth shut. The responses you receive throw you back
into an undercurrent of IT'S ALL YOUR OWN FAULT! Which
reinforces what you have been told all along by your partner.
Everything you have endured and inflicted on you was indeed
YOUR OWN FAULT.

What the receiver of this information doesn't realise is, that you are
not reporting a one-off incident, that by the time you find it
necessary to seek advice and discuss your situation, you are way
deep into a highly abusive relationship. One that is extremely
complex and multifaceted, with many intertwining layers. When it
comes to abuse it's never straight forward, black and white, it has so
many levels which are fuelled with thoughts, emotions, feelings, gut
instincts and intuition. With a belief system that has been

manufactured and manipulated by your partner in a commissive fashion to keep you compliant and submissive.

You struggle yourself to define the difference between that which is perceived normal behaviour versus that which is unacceptable. The abusive acts are minimised and normalised through time, incorporated into day-to-day life.

The way in which you are treated is drip fed over long periods of time, the balance shift and changeover is executed so gradually that you are unaware of its existence. You accept the new rules, new roles, the new behaviour, the new deliverance of consequences to your actions and adjust and readjust as the relationship develops.

Very gradually you are disempowered and moulded into complete compliance. The whole dynamics of your relationship changes with the administration of humiliation, criticism and ridicule to keep you in your place. The deviation of this is immense, impacting on every part of your being. Stripping away your uniqueness and larger than life personality until you are an empty shell filled with absolute confusion, no self-worth, no self-esteem, no self-confidence or self-belief. You are free-falling into a bottomless pit and have no hope or faith. You have long given up on the idea that things will get better and are stuck in a cycle of punishment and reward, which has no structure to it as it is forever changing. Your life consists of extreme highs or extreme lows. There is no middle ground. The outside world only ever sees the highs.

By the time you have built up the strength to open your mouth you are highly aware and have a deep understanding as to people's perception and preconceived ideas regarding domestic abuse. You know you are taking a massive risk with your disclosure and that the chances are you will be stamped with a label and branded an outcast.

At the same time amidst this free fall into the abyss you are screaming out for a lifeline, for a saviour, a protector. You're dead inside, but you don't want to die. What you are desperately looking for is someone with compassion, who is non-judgmental and who will endeavour to give you support, without criticism. In its simplest form, just listening without casting aspersions.

As the relationship grows and develops, so does the never-ending list of rules, regulations and threats. The guidelines are vague therefore open to acts of punishment if the expectations are not met. This keeps you on your toes and in a state of high anxiety as to the self-questioning of am I doing things correctly. The first rule hits you like a brick. You laugh it off initially, then become rather defensive. You are somewhat indignant and question its reason. You're not happy with it at all however the more it is repeated, the more accepting you become. Over time you realise that the first brick was merely a pebble thrown in a pond, it may have had the biggest impact however the ripples from this become larger and larger until that first rule was in fact the softest blow within the epicentre of a magnitude of rules and regulations. It will be forgotten as the ripple effect kicks into being.

The major rules are: don't tell anyone and don't ever try to leave. These come with a massive threat if breached.

So, a confession of one's life and what one is living with is a MAJOR BREACH, a MASSIVE RULE BREAKER. The consequences of this divulgence can in turn lead to considerable repercussions and if it backfires the results can be devastating. The safety of oneself and children is paramount, so when a declaration is delivered, it is done so with trust, which sadly can be diminished with one small comeback. And that is why you keep your mouth shut.

21

Over time you develop an extra sense, you become highly vigilant and attentive to the small unnoticed and overlooked details. You are on high alert and your observational skills develop to great heights. You scan for the nonverbal communication being fired off in your direction, and quickly you discover what each mean and the impact it has on you as a result. Those raised eyebrows, that look, that tap of the fingers, that shaking of the foot, the change in eye colour, the cuddle with an unhealthy grip, the stance, the posture, the sound of the door shutting, the way the car sounds as it pulls up, the sound of the door closing, the way in which a cup is placed down, words spoken through gritted teeth, the joke delivered with a nasty punchline. These are delivered both in public and in private. They are designed to send you a warning, loud and clear, without it being spelled out. This can also be a never-ending and forever-changing list. Through time this becomes your "OH FUCK" warning, warning, danger, danger list. It is of great importance when assessing situations. For your safety and the risk of your impending demise. It is imperative that you develop this skill as without it you are blind as to what is coming next.

So, my love story started off like a true romance and through time developed into a thriller/comedy/horror. It went from extreme highs to extreme lows with no middle ground whatsoever. I was either living in a pink and fluffy world or in the depths of despair. The outside world only ever saw the loved-up version with the evil being kept behind closed doors.

At 16 years of age I was stepping out of childhood and entering the big wide world. The days of school were behind me and an unconditional place at college awaited. I was in my transition phase; I was so excited about creating my future and becoming an adult.

I was the youngest of four children, a late baby. There was a large age gap between the other three and me. A mistake, or as my father put it, the best mistake he ever made. He also said I had 666 tattooed behind my ear which to this day I have never found! Our family rules were simple. Treat others as you wish to be treated yourself. Be kind. Be considerate. Respect yourself and others. Oh, and sex was for married couples and only for making babies.

The serenity prayer was our mantra:

God, grant me the serenity to accept the things I cannot change,
Courage to change the things I can,
And wisdom to know the difference.

My punishment for misbehaving consisted of a simple yet powerful sentence. "I'm disappointed in you." That was heart-breaking to hear, and the upset of those words kept me on the right track.

So, my plan was to study hard and get my diploma in nursery nursing, and travel the world working as a nanny. Have copious amounts of adventures. Meet a nice man, get married. Have three girls and one boy. Raise beautiful children, set them free in the big wide world and grow old with my husband whilst still traveling the world creating amazing memories. Sounded good to me. I was well up for it!

The week before I started college I went to stay with a friend. On the first day we went to the fair. We met a group of her friends. That's the day I met him. It was his birthday; he told me he was 18. I believed him. He was tall, exceedingly handsome, had a beautiful smile, sparkling blue eyes and a mop of blond hair. He was hilariously funny and was making everyone laugh. He referred to himself as "Leo the lion" as his birth sign was Leo. His twin sister was also there and let it slip that it was in fact their 16th birthday.

The attraction was instantaneous, he had it all going for him. He was the life and soul of the party and everyone loved him.

Even though I say it myself, I had a wicked sense of humour, I was witty, had perfectly timed one liners and delivered sarcasm with ease. I did like to swear a lot - *expressive emotive* language I called it. However, this was not a trait of my family members, so it was only delivered out with the home.

We got together really quickly; it was not in my plan but fuck me it was exciting.

At the end of our first week together as officially "going out" he told me that he loved me. I was elated. I felt so special. I couldn't believe that this fantastically amazing guy LOVED ME! How lucky was I!

Right after his declaration I received my first ever rule. DO NOT SWEAR! What the fuck! I could swear if I wanted to. I was an adult now. I put up a good argument as to why I should be free to express myself with my choice of descriptive profanities. I was dismissed and the rule was repeated and repeated and repeated. On a fuckin loop for the next 22 years!

On reflection I can see that I didn't have a very good grasp on rules nor how to uphold them as the requisition demanded.

He had plans. He was going to join the forces, travel the world. He wanted to get married, have children and create a happy family. Sounded perfect to me. He told me that he lived by a code. PRIOR

PREPARATION PREVENTS PISS POOR PERFORMANCE and that he strived for perfection in everything he did.

We had a long-distance relationship, with an hour and a half traveling time between us. We saw each other every weekend. Taking it in turn to travel to each other's homes. We spoke on the phone every night and wrote letters to each other. We were so in love. So happy. We did fun activities. We laughed all the time. We talked about everything under the sun. We would stay up all night talking. When he was tired, he had a slight turn in his eye. It was cute, a little lazy eye. We made the most of every minute and we were deliriously happy.

He told me he loved me so much. So much so that he couldn't live without me. If I ever left him, he would have no reason to live, and he would have no option but to kill himself. How lucky was I to have this guy as my boyfriend? He loved me so much!

During one of our deep and meaningful conversations he confessed to me that he had already tried to kill himself twice. He had taken overdoses.

That was it, I made it my mission to love him more than anyone else ever could. I was going to protect him, keep him safe and love him forever so that he would never have any reason to kill himself.

He started turning up at my college. I was elated to find him sitting in the refectory when I went on breaks. Then he would wait outside my classroom for the duration of that subject. Soon tutors invited him to sit in the class.

He hated being apart from me. He got to know all my college friends too. However, he wasn't very keen on me going out with them. They were distracting my studies; they were obviously not as committed to the course as I was. He thought that it was best that I declined invitations to nights out. They were a bad influence. He loved me so much and was just looking out for me. I was blessed.

On my 18th birthday he told me that I was an adult now, I could make my own decisions. I could have sex before marriage. My parents' teachings were old fashioned. If I loved him I would. After many, many, many lectures I went on the pill. We were in love. Love is forever, right.

He joined the forces and went away for his basic training. He came up on the train every weekend. Our being apart was driving him insane. He hated every minute we were apart. He cried about this on and off all weekend. My heart was breaking for him. He was telling me more frequently that if I ever left him, he would kill himself. He couldn't live without me.

My verbal reminders about not swearing had now turned into slaps, getting elbowed, tutting, and frowning.

I passed my exams with distinction. I was elated. I could now execute my plan to travel the world as a nanny. I had three interviews. One with the education department, one to nanny in Canada, and the other to nanny in Houston, Texas. I got all three jobs. Woohoo!

I accepted the post in the nursery to tide me over until my job as a nanny started. I chose Houston, for the sun and as I loved the saying "Houston we have a problem".

When I told him, he erupted and by fuck Houston, we had a major problem.

There were tears, tantrums, screaming, shouting and the reminder of what he would do if we were not together. FUCK, FUCK, FUCK! I didn't want him to kill himself, I couldn't handle the responsibility of it being my fault. I enlisted the help of my parents to sell the idea of me going away as a positive move which they approved of and promoted. They talked him round to it being a good idea. And he could visit. Right. Brilliant plan.

He hid my pill from me. Said he wanted to start a family and get married. He wanted to get me pregnant. Then I wouldn't need to go travelling. We could do it together, as a family, through the forces. I opened a new pack of pills.

He told me he was putting money away every month to visit. Guess what, the bank put all his money into an account which had the same name as him, but not his. What are the chances of that! To make matters worse it couldn't be retrieved. No savings, no visit. So, he suggested it was time I just came home. He missed me. Needed to see me. Loved me so much.

I was having the time of my life in Houston. Enjoying every minute. Without a care in the world. I was flying high; I'd never felt so free. My experience of life had grown to new levels. I was having adventure after adventure with the most amazing people. I loved every minute of it.

I came home. I was a fully-fledged real grown up adult. All independent, oozing self-confidence. I knew who I was. I had a real zest for life and living.

He met me after work. We went for a few drinks. Had a great time. Laughing, chatting, joking. As we walked in the front door of my home he started yanking at my clothes. Getting all amorous. I said no. In a flash he changed. His mood, his body language, his face. Yes, he was rather drunk, but it was as if he was a different person. His eyes changed to green, his eye turned right in. That was the instant that Leo the lion turned into Clarence the cross-eyed cunt. With his hands round my neck he lifted me straight off the floor and pinned me up against the door. I couldn't breathe. I was so scared. So confused. He was roaring and shouting but I couldn't understand any of his words. The doorbell rang. He let his grip go. I ran to the back door. I ran out. That was it. We were over. No one had ever lifted their hands to me before. He said he loved me. That's not love.

He wouldn't let up. He called me all the time. I hung up. He turned up at my door crying. He didn't get in. He wrote nice letters. He wrote nasty letters. He said he would kill himself. I didn't respond. He came with gifts. He sent my things back in tatters. I ignored him. After 3 months he called and spoke to my dad. Said he was getting married and posted to Germany. I was heartbroken. I thought he loved me.

I retrained as a croupier. Time to travel again.

A few weeks later I answered the phone without thinking. It was him. He declared his love for me. Said his relationship was a rebound. Asked if I would go back to him if he called off the wedding. I said no.

A call came from his mum. He was in the hospital. In intensive care. On a ventilator. Machines everywhere. He was in a bad way. He had a motorbike accident. He was asking for me. The consultant said to get family members in straight away. My parents advised me not to go. I went. Was this all my fault? Was it an accident? He said he would kill himself. FUCK, FUCK, FUCK!

We got engaged.

We went on holiday. We went out for a few drinks. Several drinks. Had a great night. I climbed into bed, on his side, at the wall. He was laughing and dancing around the room. It was hilarious. Next thing my face was pressed up against the wall. An Artex wall. Instant pain. I was flung across the room. Clothes ripped off me. An ashtray thrown at me which missed, hit the floor and shattered into thousands of tiny slithers of glass. My feet were cut to shreds. I was thrown out onto the balcony naked. I banged on the glass door, crying and asking to get back in. An angry Clarence the cross-eyed cunt stared back at me with so much hatred. I grabbed the swimming towels from the railings. Wrapped one round me and used the other as a cover. I was out till morning. He let me in. Said he couldn't remember a thing. It was the drink. AGAIN!

Our wedding was amazing. I felt a million dollars. Everyone enjoyed it. The whole day was lovely. Leo the lion looked at me with such loving eyes. I was so happy. We got to the honeymoon suite. The big exciting wedding night in style. We got into bed. The look of Clarence was beginning to appear. He told me this: *You're lucky I married you. You are wee, fat and ugly. You have brown hair and brown eyes. I'm attracted to tall slim blonde haired, blue-eyed, good-looking women. You are a 3, I'm a 10. I will be looking for 9s and 10s. I've done you a favour because no one else would ever look at you. I'm your first, your last and your only. If you ever go with anyone else, I will kill you. You will only be good for having my kids and having my tea on the table. You'll be faithful because you are so ugly and stupid.* Then he spent the night watching TV.

We went to Spain on our honeymoon. To his grandparents'. Single beds. I spent the two weeks going into churches looking for a priest. I wanted him to grant me an annulment of the marriage on the grounds of non-consummation. I honestly thought I could do that! I wasn't even catholic. I was Baptist. I was fuckin desperate! No joy. I was doomed!

We returned to our first married quarter, forces housing. I was given a whole new set of rules; these were forces rules. The rules and regulations to abide by were now double layered. I was given a manual on how to look after my home. Instructions with pictures, may I add, on how to hoover a carpet, strip and clean a cooker, and keep your house clean on a daily basis. The grass had to be a certain length. They could come in at any time and inspect the property, wearing white gloves, to ensure everything was spotlessly clean. So, study up, Cinderella, this has to be upheld to the letter.

Now every Friday night the forces reward their men with a "beer call". A pat on the back for a week's hard work. In essence, it was a free bar and a major piss up. So, Leo the lion would leave for work on a Friday morning and Clarence the cantankerous cunt would return. I just knew by the sound of the door opening if it was going to be a night of pure hell or if he was going to go to bed and sleep it off. The feelings of trepidation were consuming. Keeping your wife in check and boasting about how you did this was always a hot topic with his peers. Something to have a good laugh about.

I was commuting to my job. He told me to give it up. I did. I fell pregnant. It was twins. He was angry. I miscarried. I was a failure. I was useless.

I fell pregnant again. He said he wasn't the father. Must be the next-door neighbour's. Nope, it's yours. The dial went up in the arguing. The dial went up on the beatings. The dial went up on the nasty remarks. I was even fatter and uglier now. Without a job I had no income. He gave me no money. I didn't deserve it. In a rage he pushed me down the stairs. My baby!! He ran down behind me, pulled me up. Chucked me outside. He let me back in as he was going to work the next morning. I stood in a phone box all night scared and crying.

We had a daughter. The most beautiful, contented baby ever. I was feeding her. He was angry. He stated that I loved my daughter more than I loved him. I said *YES, I DO!!* I did. I loved my baby with every part of my being. He stormed out. Was gone for hours. Came back crying. I had deeply upset him. He was jealous of our baby. He told me I had to pay him more attention to make up for spending time with the baby.

We were posted. I felt more isolated. I had no friends. No family. Just the 3 of us. Alone. He was back to throwing me out. Only now he waited until the baby was down for the night. I wandered around on and off throughout the night. Had little naps on the park bench. Tried to dodge the patrolling guards. If I saw them, I would say I was out for fresh air. In the snow, in pyjamas. Right then!

I had had enough. I needed to leave. I waited until he was at work. Got a bag and put some things in it for myself and my baby. Put her in the buggy and headed to the train station. I lifted the cheque book for the fare. I was at the counter, buggy parked beside me, cheque book open, pen in hand when the buggy moved. I turned quickly. Clarence was glaring at me. One hand snatched the cheque book, the other the buggy. "You can do what you want, but she's mine, the money is mine and you're dead!" How he knew I will never know. I told no one of my plan. I went home. Things were worse. I had broken a major rule. He told me he could read my mind. I believed him.

I was given a new threat. If you leave me, I will kill you and put your daughter up for adoption. Or I might just kill the both of you.

We were posted. Another fresh start. Isolated even more. No family, no friends, no support. I fell pregnant again. He said he wasn't the father. I must be having an affair. He turned the dial up again. I was in bed sleeping. Next thing I was dragged out of bed by the hair. I hit the floor. Was dragged across the room by the hair. He was angry that I had gone to bed before him. He threw me down the stairs. I got stuck halfway, he kicked me free, then dragged me to the bottom. I was thrown through the house. He wrapped the phone cable round my throat and started choking me. He pinned me bent backwards over the kitchen worktop and held a knife at my throat. He threw me on the floor, jumped on me, kicked me, punched me. He pulled me to my feet, ripped my clothes off me and threw me naked outside. I cried. I screamed. I begged to get in. I wanted my daughter. I wanted my clothes. I wanted this to stop. He opened the door and threw my clothes at me. I quickly got dressed. I pleaded and begged to get in. He let me in. I ran upstairs to get my daughter. He grabbed her off me. There was a tug of war with my daughter. She was hysterical. I let go. I couldn't cope with her being upset. He pushed me out the room. I went downstairs. Curled up into a ball and sobbed my heart out. He came down. Threw me out. I wandered the streets. He let me in as he left for work. He gave me the silent treatment for a week. Scraped his meals straight into the bin without eating a bite.

I had another beautiful daughter. I was blessed. It was a miracle this baby made it to birth. A gift from God.

My two amazing daughters were the absolute loves of my life. I adored them. Was so in-love with them. They brought me so much joy and happiness. They kept me alive, gave me a reason to breathe.

He told me that if I ever tried to leave again, he would get a forces solicitor and go for full custody of the girls. He would win. He was the one with a steady job, the quarter was in his name, he had a good income. He was the best parent. I didn't have a leg to stand on.

He went to see his forces doctor. He booked a vasectomy. I had no knowledge of this. I did not give my consent.

We were posted. To Germany this time. Even further away from family and friends. The isolation increased. He was going away on deployment. Getting his kit ready to go. He told me to iron his shirts. He always saw to his kit himself as there was a specific way in which things were done. I was on the last shirt. He inspected the ones which I had done. He took the iron off me and put it on the side table. In a flash he tipped the ironing board. It went flying. He threw the shirts in the air. He was roaring and screaming at me. I had messed up. The shirts weren't done to perfection, to his standards. I tried to get up. I was knocked down. He kicked, he punched, he pulled me up. Threw me out in the hallway. Pinned me up against the wall by the throat. He lifted me right off the ground, both hands choking me as he banged my head off the wall at the same time. My hands were hitting the wall, my feet kicking the wall. I was above eye level with him. I couldn't breathe. I couldn't see. I was scared. I thought I would definitely die this time. Who would look after my daughters? Everything went black. I blanked out. I came round in a heap on the floor. Everything was sore, so very sore. I got up. He had finished ironing all of his shirts.

I ironed my clothes for work. I was a kindergarten manager. My girls came to work with me.

He went on another deployment. He took all the cash, the cheque book, the cash cards. I had not a penny to my name for three weeks.

We were given a house move. Still at the same camp. Another new start. I made a friend. I wasn't allowed friends. He constantly bad mouthed my friend.

We went out. We had a great time. Such a laugh. We were walking home. Talking and having a fun time. I felt a blow on my face. Was dragged into a garden. He threw me to the ground. He pinned me down. Was ripping my clothes off. I struggled to get him off me. Arms and legs everywhere. I rolled about the ground, trying to scramble to my feet, then getting knocked down again. He put one hand over my mouth, used the other to get at my clothes. His knee pinning me down. Then boom. A security light fired on. Lit up the garden like a flood light. He bounced up and ran off. I got to my feet. Stood in the garden trying to fix my clothing. I looked up at the sky. Put my arms in the air and shouted, "THANK YOU GOD!"

I was under instructions to meet him after his beer call. I thought all the wives were going. I was the only one. I was in the midst of twenty or so men. He went to the toilet. Came back. Accused me of having sex with all these men whilst he was gone. I laughed. He did not. I was marched out with a firm grip on my arm. He kicked me to the curb. Guys walked past. He screamed and roared and lashed out. He dragged me along the street, still shouting and lashing out. Marched me right out of the camp gates and towards the main road. He explained that he was going to kill me for real this time. I was wearing all black. That was perfect. He was going to throw me in front of a car, they wouldn't see me till it was too late. The road was unlit. In the middle of nowhere, outside the base perimeter. He had both my wrists grabbed tightly. He was dragging me towards the road. My feet were sliding over the surface beneath. I kept trying to pull back. I was struggling. I got one arm free. He pulled me with more force. Cars were whizzing past. He was laughing. We tussled at the roadside. There was a tug of war going on. I grabbed the handbag

34

that was swinging from my shoulder and I swung it at him. It hit the side of his head. He went down in one fell sweep. Hit the deck. Out cold. I stood over him. FUCK, FUCK, FUCK!!!! I've killed the cunt!! I always thought it would be the other way around. I stood over him consumed with fear. MY GIRLS. Shit! I needed to see them before I went to prison. I ran, ran like the wind, I had to get home to see my babies. A car drew up beside me, a guy shouted get in. I shouted *no*. Kept running. It pulled up again. I noticed it was a high ranking officer all uniformed up. He said he wanted to get me home safely. I got in the car, first time ever trusting a stranger. I didn't say a word. Only my street name. I sent the babysitter away. Locked the door. Went into my daughters' room. Just stood watching them sleeping. Silent tears rolling down my face. Then bang, the front door got kicked in. I heard him scream my name. I locked the bedroom door. He kicked it in. He went for me. I ran about the room. Got out and locked myself in the bathroom. He ripped the vent off the bottom of the door. Stuck one arm through trying to grab me. All I could see was an infuriated Clarence with rage spewing from him. I was curled up in a ball on the floor as far away from the door as possible. I started laughing. He was like "here's Johnny" from 'The Shining'. And in true horror fashion, they never stay down. I was not a murderer and I wasn't going to prison. But I might be dead soon. I'm not!

Once again, I had to make a deal with a mister-fix-it guy from the camp to do all the repairs on the quiet. A bottle of booze and cigarettes from the NAAFI.

I was sleeping. Felt a foot on my back. Then smack, I hit the floor. In a flash hands were round my throat. My head getting banged off the floor, then the wall. He bounced me off every wall. We ended up in the living room. I got up on my feet. He knocked me down. He stripped me. Threw me out the patio door into the garden. I grabbed a nightshirt from the washing line. It was my new trick. Leave clothes out overnight for emergencies. I had a pack of cigarettes stashed too and a lighter of course! I was sitting on the garden swing having a smoke when I realised that someone was out on the balcony in the next block. I said, "Hi, it's such a hot night isn't it? I'm just out for fresh air and to cool down." We started chatting. She had been woken up with someone hammering nails into the wall, strange time to hang pictures up she thought! I waited until she had gone back inside and made my way down to the cellar. I had a little corner to go to when I was thrown out. Had it hidden by empty packing boxes. I had put up his camp bed and taken his sleeping bag from his kit. Had it ready and waiting at all times.

He was having another affair. It was my friend. I had no friends anymore.

I wanted to leave. I had to ask the families officer for permission. He said no. I couldn't tell him the real reason I wanted to leave. My husband would be charged and posted. We were sent to marriage guidance. I was given instructions on what I could say and couldn't say. If I said the wrong thing, he was going to kill me and the girls. We went to the first appointment together. We were given one on one slots. Highly confidential. My appointment was first. He asked what I had disclosed. I said, "Nothing." He pinned me backwards over the kitchen worktop. Held a knife at me. Said talk. I pushed him off. I ran into the garden, scooped both my girls up from the paddling pool. One under each arm and ran like the fuckin wind. Two wet children screaming not knowing what was going on. I went to one of his boss's house. His wife played with the girls. He phoned the camp. They sent a priest out. He went to visit Clarence then came to see me. He took me to the garden to talk. The priest sat down, beer in one hand, cigarette in the other, told me my husband was fuckin crazy and needed locked up. I silently stared open mouthed at him.

36

Then I started to laugh. He asked what was funny. I said, "You're a priest, you're smoking, drinking and swearing." His reply, "It's because I'm a priest that I can do what the fuck I want!" Absolute legend. Loved him! Wish I'd met him on my fuckin honeymoon!

The girl on the balcony's husband became friends with my husband. We spent a lot of time together as couples and as families. She had two boys the same ages as my girls. I had found a true friend and a soulmate.

He was going on deployment. We all left the house together to wave him off from his pickup. He nipped back to the house alone as he had forgotten something. We waved him off. Went home. The front door was locked. The patio door was locked. I had no keys. The door was open when we left. He had his keys. I managed to bounce the hinges on the tilt and turn patio door so I could get my hand in and twist the lock to open the door. I got in. Couldn't find my keys anywhere. The buggy was in the boot of the car. He was away for 3 months! Bastard.

We were driving on the autobahn. Going really fast. He was arguing with me. He drove really close to the car in front and pulled out to overtake at the very last second. He was demonstrating his new threat. That he could have an accident that would kill me outright whilst leaving him unscathed, it was all down to timing and the positioning of the impact between cars.

My balcony friend was a hairdresser. She offered Leo an open bladed Turkish shave. He jumped at the chance. He was well pleased. There he was with the hot towels, as happy as Larry. She was standing behind him chatting away. I was standing watching. We were all having a right laugh. She lathered his face up. Asked if he was enjoying it. *YES* he proclaimed. She was up tight behind him. One hand firmly on his forehead, the other with the open blade taking its first stoke over his face. She wiped the shaving soap on the towel wrapped around him. Put the blade back on his face. She pushed his head backwards into her and leaning in she spoke to him as she slowly ran the blade from one ear to the other around his throat. She said, "If you ever lay one finger on her again, I will slit your fucking throat, you evil bastard. Got it?!" He said *YES*. I stood with my mouth hanging open, thinking, "Oh fuck, I'm dead!" She let her grip go, moved the blade, he jumped up, ran to the bathroom and locked himself in. We laughed and laughed but didn't say a word.

Things were fine. Then we got posted again. Another move. Back to the beginning again.

He was drinking every night. Leo had vanished. Clarence was larger than life. I started drinking too. It wasn't so sore when I was filled with alcohol.

We were out on camp one night. I saw a girl crying. I went to talk to her. Said, tell me it all, I won't remember, I'm drunk. She poured her heart out. My advice - leave that bastard, why are you putting up with that, I wouldn't! We became best friends.

My balcony friend arrived at the same camp a year later. We all got on great. We made more friends. Soon we had a circle of friends.

We were all at a house party. My best friend and I ended up in the bathroom having a deep and meaningful conversation. We were putting the world to rights. Then we hear him shout my name, he was banging on the door, demanding I opened the door. He was angry. We were scared. We didn't know what to do for the best. He started kicking in the door. I was pushing against the door. My best friend was over in the corner. He was going to kill me. She came up with an idea. Jump out the window. It's the only way out. Seemed like the safest option, even though we were upstairs. I could make the jump no problem, right. She took over holding the door back as it rattled in its frame with every blow he gave. I made a leap for the window. He burst in. My best friend went flying, she tried to stop her fall by holding onto the towel rail and ripped it right off the wall in her free fall, landing in a heap at the side of the toilet. I had one hand on the window handle, one half of me outside and was just about to leap when he grabbed my hair and dragged me backwards. I flew through the air and landed in the bath. Clutching out in mid-flight, I had grabbed onto the shower curtain. It was now entwined with me and the shower pole in the bath. He was going berserk. The bathroom was trashed. Another fix-it job was needed.

The men were all at a beer call. Myself and five friends gathered at my house. All the kids were in the living room having a movie night with snacks and juice. We were in the dining room with music and drink. He came in. Clarence in all his glory. He was not happy. He demanded everyone leave. We laughed. He flipped. CD player was hurled across the room, everyone stopped singing and jumped to their feet, getting out of the way. It was a good song too. Cher's "oh no not my baby!" He was arguing. He was getting shouted back at. He went for me. He was confronted. He went for a friend, then another. Scattering things and women all over the place. The children were hysterical. Two friends took the majority of the children away, out of the house. One took my oldest daughter and ran. My younger daughter was asleep on the couch and the only child left. The fighting went all through the house. He hit one friend so hard that she flew through the air, hit the wall with so much force that she slid down it. I screamed at her to run. She did. My balcony friend and I remained. We tried to protect each other. We ended up back in the dining room. Trying to pull him off each other. I told her to get my daughter out of the house and run, I would hold him off. She told me to do it and she would hold him off. It was absolute chaos and carnage. She ran out with my daughter in her arms, still asleep. I took my last hit from him and ran, ran like the fuckin wind. He was on our tail. A quick look round and he was catching up. We passed a minibus dropping off guys from camp. They tried to stop him. We kept running. He fought all three. We got into her house. One friend was already there with her boys. My oldest daughter wasn't there, nor the friend that got her out. I was hysterical, where was my baby. We locked the front door just as he tried to get in. He was raging. He smacked himself up against the living room window, pounding on it, demanding he get in, demanding he get his children. Then it went quiet. He vanished. At the same time, we looked at each other and shouted *FUCK, the back door!* We ran through the house. Got it bolted just in time. He kicked the fuck out the door. SILENCE. He was gone. We looked out the windows and couldn't see him. We started phoning around our friends to find my missing daughter. No joy. More crying. The guys had radioed the forces police. Someone had phoned the civilian police. The place was crawling with police. He gave them all the run around. Was being chased like something out of the keystone cops. Up lanes, over fences, through gardens, on the road, off the road. He was jumping onto the road and shouting to the forces police, "you can't touch me, I'm on civvy land," then jumping into gardens shouting to the civilian police, " you can't touch me, I'm on crown property," running around giving them all the slip. The civilian police caught him. Put him in their van. It was swaying from side to side, he was pounding on the inside, screaming he had rights and to let him out. The forces police came with my friend and daughter. They had been taken to the guard room. We were interviewed by the forces police. They told me that if I pressed charges, they would charge me. I did not press charges. He was kept in the civilian cells all weekend. At court on the Monday morning the forces police took over before the case was called. He was charged with three counts of assault and breaking the nose of one.

He kicked off. He was sectioned. Was in a psychiatric hospital. It was all my fault. His boss came to see me. I said I was leaving him. He said he would take me to tell him. Best place for him to be for that kind of news, he would be supported through this harsh blow that I was giving him in his time of need. We went. I told him. He cried. He got angry. I left. I got dropped off at the shop. Took my time going home. His workmate drove past me, stopped and told me to get in the car. Said everyone was out looking for me. A search party was out. What the fuck was going on?! He took me home. There were 22 messages on my answering machine. He had escaped, or some bright spark in their infinite wisdom had released him. He was known to be walking the 8 miles home. I was to call the guard room for instruction. I was told to open my front and back door wide. That the next-door neighbour, a policeman, would be sitting on his doorstep polishing his shoes. That out the back two other neighbours of high ranks would be out cutting their grass and chatting over the fence. That there would be two police cars hidden out of sight round each corner. The families worker was on her way. I was to get my children to a safe place. I did as I was told. He came. He erupted. He was taken away.

I moved to a different camp. To an excess quarter. I was given an eviction notice after 92 days. I was no longer a dependent. My rent tripped. He found me.

I moved house. He found me.

He went to military prison. They asked me to give a good character statement. I declined.

I moved house.

He got early release for good behaviour.

He found me.

He told me he was rehabilitated. Stopped drinking. Done anger management. He pleaded and pleaded with me to give it another go. I said no.

He came out the forces. Had nowhere to go. Asked if he could move in for a bit until he found a place. He needed to be near his children.

Leo was back. We gave it another go. We bought a house. A beautiful big four-bedroom house. Clarence made his return.

Last straw. It was over. I wasn't allowed to leave until I had somewhere decent to take his children. I was sleeping in the spare room.

He bought me twelve red roses. I was perplexed. Hated red roses. To me they signified death. He went upstairs. He had taken an overdose. I phoned my mum to come look after my girls. She asked if the ambulance was there yet. FUCK, FUCK, FUCK! I hadn't phoned them yet. I was so focused on my girls being looked after I hadn't done it! My mum came. The police came. The rapid response paramedic came. The ambulance came. He told them all that it was my fault. That I was leaving him. To hospital we went. My best friend came to the hospital. He thanked her for coming. She looked at him then said, "I'm not here for you, I'm here for her!" We laughed. He didn't.

He came home. Clarence was not happy. He was arguing. He was roaring. He went for my oldest daughter, I jumped in between, he went for me, she jumped in between, it repeated several times. The room got trashed. He stormed off. We grabbed a few things, filled black bags with essentials and ran.

We went into refuge with Women's Aid.

We got a house. He found us.

We moved again. He found us.

I stopped running and started hiding.

Hid in the house for twelve years. My prison. I was agoraphobic and claustrophobic. I had severe depression, anxiety and PTSD and was an insomniac. I had already been referred to the pain management department before I left him and was being seen by a pain physiotherapist. I had several block sessions with psychologists for CBT treatment. I continued this treatment periodically but made no progress. My conditions were becoming progressively worse. My mind, my body, my home all became my prison. After eleven years of being away I hit a brick wall. Physically and mentally. I was extremely ill. I thought I was dying. I was on my way out. I couldn't walk, couldn't hold my head up, couldn't swallow. The pain was horrific. I had given up 99% with 1% self-preservation remaining.

I was sent to numerous consultants to get to the bottom of my devastating illness. I was seen by a neurologist, a rheumatologist, a gynaecologist, a urologist, a bowel surgeon, a facial surgeon, an oral surgeon, a heart specialist, ear nose and throat specialist, a psychiatrist, a psychologist, a psychiatric nurse, the pain clinic physiotherapist once more. They did blood tests, X-rays, scans, CT scans, MRIs, nerve conductance tests. With each test more diagnoses. Neurological illnesses and autoimmune diseases galore. However, as each result came back, I was asked the same question over and over by each and every person that was dealing with me. "Have you ever been the victim of domestic abuse." It had all come back to haunt me with vengeance. The damage to my mind, my

43

body, my soul had left a permanent mark. Damage to my bones, my tissue, my nerves. From the inside out. A permanent husky voice to boot. It's so painfully sore on so many different levels.

I received two years of intense treatment. The fix-it team consisted of a psychiatric nurse, a pain psychologist, and my existing pain physiotherapist. My physiotherapist reintroduced me to having faith and hope for the future. She worked hard at my repair. She brought me back to life. She became my higher power.

At one appointment she gave me a leaflet for Saje Scotland. I was still in a bad way but decided to give it a try. By this time, I had been away twelve years. Was it going to help? Was I taking the place of someone who desperately needed it?

I went. The facilitator said, "This course will change your life." I thought, will it fuck! She told us we could swear. I smiled. She told us she understood and had been through abuse. Had been in a bad way. Had done the Saje courses. She became my hero.

I had always felt so isolated and didn't tell anyone for fear of being outcast. I had now met a group of women who had been through the same, who didn't judge, who understood. I had now found a sense of peace and acceptance. I learnt that this was not my fault, I began to let go of my shame, my guilt, my fear and I entered the grief process.

Now realising that my treatment had been administered through choice for power and control. That once you stripped back each individual's unique experiences there was an underlying commonality of tactics and traits that linked types of abuse.

So, I broke the rules. I swore, I smoked, I snored, I farted, I laughed, I smiled, I sang, I said no, I cut my hair, I had a career, I furthered my education, I made friends, I talked non-stop. What can I say, I'm a rebel. However, it didn't grant the punishment I received.

The outside world only saw a loved-up couple. A loving family. A husband who was kind and considerate. A guy who climbed the ranks and was an expert in his field, who went everywhere with his wife. A wife who worked, who went back to study and changed fields to become a social care team manager. A strong independent woman. They saw a happy home that was spotless, with expensive furniture and the latest in all technology. A top of the range car. Happy family holidays. Meanwhile I was living a split life. Perfection personified.

I have met THE most amazing people. Women who have lived through abuse and are now empowering so many more. Changing lives. Mentors, heroes, guides, enablers, promoters, confidantes.

To date I have had:
16 years of self-discovery and empowerment.
22 years of role play with an ever-changing script.
12 years of self-destruct, stuck in a cycle of guilt, shame and fear.
2 years in recovery and rehabilitation.

I've gone from SORE to SOARING.

Whilst Clarence is still ROARING.

With a realisation that life is for living and living it with FREEDOM is a must!

JOY

THIS IS ME

We met in Primary School aged four and a half so we knew each other for what seemed like forever.

He is on every Primary School photograph staring out at me among my memories.

I had a happy, loving, supportive childhood with an indulgent and overprotective Mother as I am an only child, so was spoiled as much as my parents could afford.

High School and College followed as night follows day. I was never academically gifted but worked hard and passed in the top classes. I suppose I did better in the subjects I liked and the personality of the teachers and lecturers helped as I now know I sought praise for achievements.

I moved to Edinburgh as the government department I worked for was based there. This seemed a huge freedom for someone from a village and an overprotective Mother. I had a great social life and many friends but went home each weekend. Of course, that's when I met up again with my future husband.

He phoned everyday while I was away and always waited for me as the train arrived home. Little did I realise that this was so he knew exactly where I was. I thought it was love. Many more instances of control and isolation were to follow but all the while I fell for the line they all use. "I love you and just want to keep you safe."

The more my Mum tried to put me off him the more I rebelled and trusted that he really wanted me. Mums sometimes do know best!

After a few months he started pleading with me to give up my job and get one nearer home. Again a control thing I didn't recognise. I was thrilled he wanted to see me every night instead of just weekends.

The new job was OK but not as satisfying as the one in Edinburgh and of course I lost my circle of friends there.

We got married and that's when things began to change from loving and caring to real control.

Friends started to ask me to go out less and less as I would arrange to go and then because he made such a fuss or downright stopped me from going I would not turn up. Classic signs of control.

Two wonderful children followed but increasingly I became afraid of the moods and the silent treatment sometimes along with violence. I had never experienced any of this before him and with two young kids to cope with I suppose it all made me more subservient than ever.

Money was never a problem and I was never questioned about any spending. He was a hard worker but of course this meant long absences from home and even while working at home his hours were long.

The kids and I were free to do what we wanted but when time came for his return everything and I mean everything, had to be "perfect". House like a show house, car serviced and full of fuel, fridge and cupboards full of food he liked, all bills paid. If the duvet cover wasn't the same one as when he left it meant that I had been having an affair in his eyes. You couldn't make this up.

He would arrive home bearing expensive toys and huge bars of chocolate for the kids, perfume for me along with gold jewellery. Nothing but the best for his family. Of course outsiders and indeed, initially, my family thought how lucky I was to have such a husband.

When the violence ramped up I would be given "sorry" presents. Expensive jewellery and clothes. When folk would say how lucky I was I just wanted to tell them that there was a price to pay for all these luxuries. No one suspected the truth or if they did they said nothing as they relied on him fixing practical things for them, either himself or his contacts.

If I was showing any signs of violence i.e. black eyes or bruising I had to stay upstairs out of sight if people came to the house. Not make a sound. Couldn't even go to the loo in case I flushed it and they heard. Folk thought I had a great time away out on my own when in fact I was like Anne Frank, hidden away.

When my second child started school I had too much time on my hands to think and so I suggested I could go back to work. This was a surprisingly quiet period of control and violence. He was away for even longer periods and seemed calmer when at home. Cannabis might have something to do with this but I was so naïve about all things to do with drugs, I just hoped that we had turned a corner and things were going to be better.

So now I was coping with a full time, responsible job with an international company plus all of the aforementioned stresses of keeping the house and kids just so during his work contracts. *Walking on eggshells all the time* is an apt description of my life.

As the moods and the violence increased so the gifts became even more luxurious. Holidays arranged at the drop of a hat when he gave no thought to me having to arrange time off. A beautiful top of the range sports car for me. The insurance for this was extremely high, as we were so young, the garage questioned if we could afford it. Meals out where nothing was too much to order even if the kids weren't that hungry. They had to sit and behave.

I now see how the kids were affected, as they played up when I was on my own with them but were quiet and well behaved when their dad was at home. So this meant I was the one dishing out any discipline and he was daddy bountiful. Bad Father? Well to the outside world no, but now it's obvious that this was yet more control.

Some contracts before the children started school meant that we could rent a cottage near the workplaces. Again I thought it was because he wanted us near him but in fact it meant he knew where I was and what we were doing and of course yet more isolation from friends and family. This meant long hours on my own, knowing no one and very little time to spend together due to the contract completion time frame.

The violence sometimes erupted with no warning, no prior arguments just explosive.

At home ended up in hospital with a split in my forehead, couldn't see to drive there so a neighbour took me. The doctor wanted to remove my blood covered clothes but I remember screaming not to do that as he would see the bruises from the week prior.

The neighbour went to the house to confront him and I warned him that my husband had guns he used for rabbit, game and pigeon shoots.

Later the neighbour told me that he had never been so frightened in all his life as seeing my ex staring at him with a tight band across his nose that used to turn white with anger. Of course, this was the first time anyone had confronted him about his behaviour towards me. The cat was out of the bag so to speak.

The scar I have on my forehead reminds me of just how bad things had gotten and I had been guilty of allowing it to happen. What was I thinking? My confidence was now so low I couldn't dare challenge him.

Work was my only escape but I had to turn down the promotions I was offered on a couple of occasions, again lack of confidence, as that meant I wouldn't have such regular hours and would be working with mostly men! Imagine? How was I supposed to have the energy to be up to no good with MEN?

There are a million and one small incidences of physical and mental abuse I could recall but these would be painful for me and boring for you to read about.

The one that stands out of course, and I hope that you never have to face this, is when one of the guns I mentioned was pushed under my chin with his finger poised on the trigger. The argument had once again erupted for no particular reason. Some imagined misdemeanour on my part no doubt. I had no idea if it was loaded or not. The bruises the gun left were obviously of the two barrels and the gun sight. I knew I had to get out of there or he would kill me. Each gun as deadly as the other.

Imagine watching the end of a film and when he comes home and says he's going to bed, you say I'll be up in a few minutes when the film finishes. All OK no obvious problems. You get into bed and he seems to be asleep. You turn out the light and then he explodes. Lifting the bed up and tipping you out onto the floor and smashing your face with the ceramic bedside lamp. Pulls the wardrobe over on top of you so you can't get out or up. All of this with no explanation or seeming reason except you didn't go up to bed immediately. My nose was broken by the lamp and a young guy in my office on seeing me the next morning was so shocked he drove me into the hospital to have it straightened before it set. One of the most painful things I ever endured. No one else questioned what had happened to me.

Despite the new house, the new kitchen, the money, the cars and luxury sorry presents I knew I had to get out or I'd die. There was no in between. Reporting him to the police would only make things worse. Once you cross him there is no going back, no forgiveness. I witnessed this with how he was with other people. Folk were afraid of him, even grown men. A guy who had been my life-long friend made a mistake at work where my ex was his boss. Ex pulled the entire fixture off the wall in temper and sent it crashing to the floor. The guy had never witnessed anger like this before, told me he was terrified and of course our friendship cooled noticeably.

My escape wasn't dramatic, but too specific to record here. (Easily identifiable).

I was able to use money I had stashed from my salary to rent and furnish a flat and buy a not so flash car as I was used to. Changed days, but I could close the door at night and not worry about being attacked verbally or physically. Peace reigned.

Work became so much easier as I had less to worry about domestically. This makes it all seem easy but I had the advantage of money and a secure well paid job.

Not everyone has these advantages and that must make escape, because that is what it is, so much more difficult.

Today I am happy and free with a loving family and a wonderful supportive husband who has never asked about what went on in my previous marriage and accepts that I really don't want to recall these times. He knows I am strong and overcame it on my own. You can after time, start to forget but you can never forgive and any small thing can trigger a feeling of panic even though he is nowhere near.

If you have never been subject to or witnessed domestic abuse it is hard for anyone to understand why you just don't leave. Well I hope I've explained why.

After all of the above, all I can say is **<u>"THIS IS ME"</u>**. Accept me for who I am and the life I've had, or go to hell.

FIGHTING AGAINST
THE DESOLATION OF ME

He walked into the room, full of charm and smiles. There was an instant connection between us. He liked everything that I liked, he had done the same things as me. It was like a dream come true. He said he loved me a week after we met. He told me of his ex-girlfriend who had treated him badly and the mummy who never gave him cuddles. He got my sympathies and affection. He showered me with attention, gifts, took me places, all the things I craved were missing from my life.

Then the changes came, subtle and slow, meant to cause distress, but only in incessant drips that infiltrate your mind and drive you crazy trying to understand what is going on! Gaslighted.

Then only a few short weeks later, he told me that his family had described me as a gold digger: I was only interested in him because he had a car, he had a job, I wanted to use him for these things. His mum was concerned that I had children and was looking for a daddy for them. I looked old and haggard, I was rude and unapproachable, and I was unfriendly. They had never met me at this point; they knew nothing of me other than what he had told them. He said I should write to his mum, assure her of my intentions. Foolishly I did. I wrote to her telling her I would never hurt her son or use him in any way. He reminded me this of daily for a while and then only in later disagreements.

I used to visit my mum every day, take her shopping or help her with things she needed done, but he resented this. He resented my relationship with her, the closeness we had and that we did things for each other. He would complain to me every day when I got home about the time I spent at my mum's, until such time as I was seeing her only maybe once or twice a month; this was a dramatic change to our relationship. He hated that she had a relationship of sorts with my ex-husband. He was jealous of the time they had together, time spent supporting her and me through the death of her husband, moving homes, visiting family and friends. Eventually he moved me hundreds of miles across the country, isolating me further, so the contact I had with my mum and family was by telephone and occasional visits.

My friends didn't like him. They visited once or twice after we got together, but then stopped coming. He would tell me they were jealous of us and our relationship, what we had together. I believed him; I was living in a love bombing shell. They tried to warn me, they tried to get my attention but I couldn't see or hear them.

I had a volunteer role as a special constable. He used this as a way to "get him off" with bad behaviours in the local area. He humiliated me whilst I was on duty by running up and kissing me in front of my section lead. I was told off for this. He went on the radio ranting about the treatment of special constables. I had to drop out; it was impossible to attend and support the service I had volunteered to. I had lost my support network. He was incredibly jealous of the relationships I had especially with male officers. I gave up on this role despite it being important to me.

I was an assistant swimming teacher at our local club. Years of fundraising to get a local pool, and here we were, clubs, lessons everything was put in place. I had supported fundraising and wanted to support the pool and the kids locally. I signed up and trained to be a teacher, I went every week. Kids called me the witch for making them work too hard, even my own kids chanced their luck. But this was something he didn't like; he didn't want me doing anything that took me away from giving him attention. He made it impossible, complaints, moaning, put downs, until eventually there was no option but to give in to his demands and have some internal peace.

He took out credit cards and built up thousands of pounds of debts, unsecured loans that he never paid a penny to and eventually a secured loan, all attached to the family home. The safety and security of my children was put at risk when he failed to pay or make arrangements to pay any of the debts. It turned out that the secured loan that he failed to pay was because he had been accused of sexual assault in his workplace and had been suspended. He lied and covered it up. Everyone was his enemy; everyone was out to get him. He got offered to "leave" the job he was in or be sacked. His record recorded the allegations, but the poor victim, he said she was crazy, friendless, looking for attention, spreading vicious rumours about him. He was always the victim of others, committing crimes against people and blaming them, hated by his managers, stitched up by his colleagues, set up to fail.

During my pregnancy and after the birth of our son, there were many degrees of emotional abuse. From him and his parents, they were taking the child away, taking him to schooling near them, giving up work to look after him, an abundance of events that caused great upset. I was told by the best friend of the family that I should leave whilst I could, go back to Wales to my own family because they were taking my son away from me. This caused great anxiety and worry. Why would they want to do this? I was having nightmares on a daily basis, couldn't sleep, and couldn't settle. I was constantly troubled by this and worried about the outcome of having a baby with him. OK, my son would be their grandchild, but he was my child and decisions about his life were in our hands not that of the grandparents.

He would not stand up to his parents; he refused to put in boundaries to protect our son or me. He despised any kind of boundaries, believed that between people in a relationship, boundaries weren't required, and he had no respect for boundaries that weren't even his own.

Also after the birth of my son, and subsequent post-natal depression episode, he decided that I was not engaged enough on his needs so he signed up to numerous dating web sites. Not just the standard ones either, but websites to engage in group sex or bondage and such like. He paid for some of these sites, too. After I found them he denied having engaged with anyone, but it was obvious. There were receipts for hotels for two people or more, there were days he was missing, unable to contact, lost his phone, left his phone on a train, excuses were endless, and obviously I eventually learned about failures with bills and loaning money from payday lenders, etc.

He would use his female colleagues in all jobs to cause triangulation. Having sexually explicit chats with them, making it very clear they were more than friends and that given any opportunity he could go off with any of them. This happened repeatedly, sometimes with more than one colleague at a time. However, it always turned out that it was me that had the problem. I was paranoid, I was foolish, I was the one who was abusive because I was finding and actively searching out the reason for the games he played. His behaviour always changed when he had his newest conquest, his newest toy to use in the triangulation. I never ever identified what it was, but something changed, something was different and this thing always set off some desire in me to find out what was happening, it was as if a switch was flicked and I knew he was engaging in this method of control and I would become the victim of this exploitation. I worried too that I was abusive, that my behaviours were actually abusive, and thankfully with the support of Saje Scotland I learned that this was not the case.

He would play games that lasted years, games that involved people, games that involved money, games that involved care and support for family. I was to wear makeup, then not wear makeup because I was just flirting with male colleagues. I only did myself up to get the interest of the doctors or the clothes that I wore were only for them to be able to ogle at me. Work was uncomfortable, I would hide behind doors trying to speak to the consultant, be on edge checking to see if he was looking at me in a sexual way, terrified that this was the case. If I spoke to males outside, i.e. travelling on a train, they would only talk to me because of my boobs, or they just wanted to have sex with me. I wasn't a person worthy of conversation or polite chit chat; it was always just about some kind of sex. I stopped talking to people; I couldn't look anyone in the eye and chat to them.

Then in 2007, he raped me, he forced himself on me and raped me despite my protests and tears. It felt wrong, but how could it be rape, he was always so against rape and assault, I kept quiet, I didn't fully understand what had happened and I shut down. I got pregnant, I wanted an abortion, and he ran in to the clinic at the last minute saying we should keep the baby, it wasn't what I wanted, and I didn't want to get rid of a child. It went against my most deeply held values; I needed to understand why I was there. I gave birth to my daughter; nearly 6 weeks early, she was tiny on 5lbs. I couldn't connect with her, I struggled to hold her, she cried constantly, I did not know what was happening to me, or why I was like this with my baby.

Rape happened again a year later. We went away for a night to a hotel. We were engaged in sexual activity, but I started to feel ill, like I was going to vomit, I begged him to stop repeatedly, all he did

58

was wrap the duvet around my head and carry on penetrating me until he had cum. He told me it felt extremely erotic to be shagging me while I was vomiting into the duvet. I bled that night too; I must have been bruised and battered inside.

Sexual mistreatments carried on, demands to engage in swapping games or dogging. I had to promise him I would do these things. He would search and find places and people to go to. Fortunately, it never quite got off the ground. He would try to engage sexual intercourse or foreplay whilst our young children were in our marital bed. I would freeze as he touched me; try to engage my child so that they did not notice what was happening. In the end, the only feasible solution was for me to get out of bed the second I heard the children stir, then as time went on, I knew the children would seek me out, if I wasn't in bed, they would come to me wherever I was, so I would get up and go downstairs early, it felt the safest option for us all.

I was always told I made all the decisions about everything in our lives, but this confused me, because I would look around and say in my head, I did not decide on that, it was chosen for me, if not by him, then by his mother. I couldn't decide on my own car, I was questioned about spending my own income, spending money on my children and helping to support my older children in moving away from home. I was to live my life under one set of rules that prevented me from having real relationships with my family, children and friends, whilst he lived under another set of rules that allowed him to be supported by his parents, to go out with his friends, to spend his money and wages on what he wanted to. He took me to the GP for medication demanding that I be put on anti depressant tablets so I would become numb and unable to think clearly about what was happening to me, he would take me and collect me from counselling sessions then criticise what had been discussed or happened and call them fools for what they said or suggested. He hated that they were making suggestions to change, or to try and get me to see what was happening in my life and how I was being manipulated and controlled. They were the ones trying to break down the barriers and help me see what was going on.

Then the seeds started to grow, the light started to shine through and break down the barriers that I had put in place to suppress the gut feeling of wrong. I knew there was something improper happening, but I couldn't quite determine what it was. I was going to the counsellor and on the way in one day I picked up the leaflet for Saje Scotland. It stood out on the shelf because it said "what is domestic abuse". I had it in my hand when I went into the room and the counsellor said that she was going to suggest I attend the programme. I thought she was joking but we talked about stuff and she said throughout our time together she felt that I was in an abusive relationship. I said, but you have heard only my side of the story, how can you know this. I didn't take it on at this point, but I had the leaflet in my handbag and it occasionally came to the top and prompted thought about the situation I was living in.

Then another person, a psychologist, said the same thing and finally, after attending Relate for relationship counselling, this counsellor who seen us both said the exact same thing and that is when the hammer truly hit home. Now I knew for sure. This counsellor had seen us both together and she could identify the controlling emotional, financial, and sexually abusive behaviour he targeted towards me.

It became exceptionally hard to ignore it; I knew something needed to change. I started to challenge his words, challenge his behaviours, I didn't accept the accusations of being a racist, or being a prude, I wasn't unapproachable, I wasn't miserable and unfriendly, I knew that I had had friends before, so why didn't I now. I knew that I had tried to invite friendships in to my life, but had had all of them destroyed by his behaviours, being sexually explicit to friends, leaving the room when people came in, making inappropriate remarks about people's attire, they didn't want to come back, and I was too ashamed to invite them.

After yet another triangulation episode, I ended our relationship in the September of the year, but it dragged slowly through to December where the final act was played out in front of everyone and people could all see the monster that hid under the charm and charisma.

I lost a lot during my relationship with him. I lost myself, I lost connection to my family, some of which can never be repaired. I lost friends. I lost jobs, I lost security in myself, I lost belief in myself, I lost my personality, I lost my trust, I lost my self esteem. He desolated me, completely isolated me from a life, he caused depression, he made me miserable. I was alone, in a bleak and gloomy life, fighting and inventing lies to conceal the truth that lay under what the outside world could see.

Now after having gone through the courses Saje offer, and volunteering for them, I am getting fixed. I am finding my own way again, redeveloping my own opinions and reinstating my own values and morals. I will never allow anyone take these things away from me again.

Thank you to Saje Scotland for providing this group, for supporting women like me and for understanding that abuse occurs side by side with what we present to the outside world. For opening eyes to the layers of relationships and what people hide under a cover of smiles and pretence.

Everyone should learn the concepts of domestic abuse through Saje's perspective. It should be instilled in our education years, where influences are highest and ideas about right and wrong in relationships can be encouraged and, with determination, changes begin before abuse comes into being.

FAITH

HOUSEHOLD BAST*RD

I think if he had hit me, I might have seen it sooner
But a clever man he was, He kept his hands to himself
Accentuating the demons around us;
Who lashed out and beat those poor girls.

I'm not a violent person, he would say every day,
I would never hit a woman; But hitting wasn't necessary,
When control was what he craved.

Look how he treats your sister, see what that man does to your mum
That's abuse that is, That's what abusive men do
I don't do that, You're lucky to have me.

Don't listen to your mum, your sisters or your friends
For jealousy prompts their pleas,
we are the perfect couple; Though no one else agrees.

People came into our lives, Friends I tried to make
Degradation was his tactic; They never came back

So many other women, all used to play his games
Triangulation and taunting, That I could easily be replaced

I had to improve my attention, I had to give more time to him
He wasn't one for sharing, Though that line was very shaded

He stole from me my family, He took away my home,
He left me with so little, While appearing the charming gentleman.

No one could hear the whispers, or see the eyebrow raise,
No one knew the triggers or warnings that were imposed.

I had to lock my mouth shut, Speak only as he deemed fit
I wasn't worth a conversation,
Forbidden to engage without his consent

People saw the material side of life, and thought that all was perfect
Yet life was intolerable and defined by hidden sadness

The shadows tried to warn me, Shouting out in my dreams
Your life is wrong – can't you see, This isn't how it's meant to be.

He wasn't Mr Charming, His tongue lashed out abuse
Behind closed doors he treated all, As toys for him to mock

He was a household bast*rd, that outside the door,
no one else could see
Damaging all around him, in his quest for grandiose vanity

I managed to escape, though that was on his terms
He had to find his new supply, to accept that I could be free.

Freedom found its way to me, by learning what he had done
Freedom saved me from his wrath
And Freedom keeps me strong.

DARING

There I was at 32. I owned a flat in Edinburgh and had a professional career. I was making a good recovery from an eating disorder which had plagued me during my teens and twenties. I was starting to feel liberated, positive and proud of myself.

I was part of a Buddhist peace movement and most weekends, I was engaged in Buddhist activities with my lovely supportive friends. I travelled extensively and was able to support many people. I felt spiritually empowered and my life was moving forward at a fast pace.

Only one thing was missing... I wanted to get married and have a family.

THEN... I met Steven...

I invited him out to a pub (a very daring step for a woman in the early 80's) and we seemed to get on like a house on fire. On reflection, I don't think he was so keen on me. I think I did all the running initially. I thought we were the perfect match and I had fallen head over heels in love.

Did I think he had any faults at all?

Well... I DID notice that he seemed to have ALMOST NO friends! This was a slight concern which I pushed to the back of my mind then although the therapist I was still seeing occasionally for my eating disorder did frown and say *hmmmmm* when I told her.

Any other anomalies I managed to ignore or dismiss.

Fast forward a year or so...

Steven said that I was so involved in Buddhism that he could not see marriage with me working. I was devasted. The very basis for my spiritual empowerment which was propelling my life forward, he found unacceptable! We therefore stopped seeing each other and I felt absolutely devastated.

My parents were also deeply disappointed and could not understand why I would give up the chance of marrying a man they really liked.

At this stage, I will remind you that all this was happening in the early 80's when it was expected that couples got married and an unmarried couple living together was still quite shocking, at least in the small town where my parents lived. Isn't it wonderful how things have changed!

After much parental persuasion and because I missed Steven so much, I wavered, phoned him and told him I had decided to give up Buddhism.

This was the hardest decision I had EVER made but I wanted to marry him so much. As time went on, I felt empty and unhappy deep in the core of my life but euphoric on the surface at the thought of getting married.

I remember several occasions where I felt broken-hearted because Steven would stop speaking to me for days over something very trivial. I implored him, begged him, saying that I was sorry and would not do it again.

I now realise, I was losing myself and although it looked on the surface as if my life was moving forward, the opposite was actually true.

We married when I was 35. His pattern of not speaking for days continued and I was plunged into emotional despair. I buried my true feelings and enjoyed the times when he was in a good mood.

During my pregnancy with our first child, I was so unhappy and missed my spiritual practice of chanting so much that I started doing it again it in secret. I felt myself regaining my old positivity and by the time our son was born, I felt much better although there was always the anxiety of being found out. When our son was three months old, I plucked up courage to tell Steven what I was doing and why I absolutely needed to do this to build up my self-esteem again.

Well, I had never seen him so angry. He moved out of our bedroom immediately and ignored our son and me for a week. Finally, when I could stand this silent treatment no longer, I said we should talk. The upshot was that I persuaded myself to give Catholicism a try as Steven had been brought up as a Catholic. His attitude changed immediately at this and we had a lovely romantic reunion.

I ended up joining the Catholic church. I used it as a substitute for my previous belief but it was actually completely different and I did not really regain my self-confidence.

By the time I was forty, we had four children. I cannot believe that I gave birth four times between the ages of 35 and forty. Looking back, I think being pregnant and having four children in rapid succession helped give me a reason for living and filled up the emptiness inside. I also felt it was something I was good at, which boosted my rapidly dwindling lack of confidence.

I was also helped by having a wonderful mother-in-law. I think she acted as a buffer in many situations. Not that she ever took sides, but her presence took the heat out of many a situation as she spent a lot of time with us. Living nearby, she would come down in the morning and she had a wonderful relationship with all our children.

We lived in a big house which Steven spent many years refurbishing. He had many skills and everyone marvelled at his handiwork. Unfortunately, this work took so long that we spent the first ten years of family life with cardboard on the floor instead of carpets and with paint peeling from the walls. My parents were quite alarmed at this and donated some money for Steven to replace the tin cupboards in our kitchen with proper units and we finally had a nice modern kitchen.

Not that I was in charge of the kitchen. Steven loved to do the shopping and plan our meals and I would heat up what he laid out for me. When I later went back to work, he came home before I did and prepared the meals. I must admit this suited me quite well as I was exhausted after a day's teaching. I was exhausted by the life I had built.

I adored our four children and they were my reason for keeping going. I also adored Steven... when he was being nice to me...

Unfortunately, he was very harsh and discouraging with the children and they suffered frequently from unfair physical and emotional punishment. Whenever I said something to him about this, he turned the blame round on me and I felt powerless to stand up for them. To my great shame, I am aware that my children were not consistently happy at home. No one in the house was, although when we went to church, we marched along the road with the father at the head as if we were a perfect family. Far from it!

69

During a family holiday, a serious incident occurred. Steven was so angry with the children, particularly my daughter who was 13, that he grabbed her, shook her and it looked as though he was strangling her as she lay on the ground. When we got home, I told a friend about this incident, I was so concerned. My friend asked me about Steven's behaviour with the children and advised me to report it immediately. By then the atmosphere in our house was becoming unbearably tense. I decided to speak to my GP. He took me very seriously and wrote down verbatim a report of what I was saying.

I felt I had betrayed my husband by speaking out about his behaviour. At the same time, this situation could not go on. My two eldest daughters had the courage to rebel and when I told Steven I had reported him, he agreed that he would no longer be physically violent with the children.

This was replaced by outrageous verbal abuse, particularly of my eldest daughter. Social services became involved and we went through children's panels and family counselling.

When I fell and broke my back, potentially disastrous and painful as it was, this was the turning point our family needed.

When I got home from hospital and things were as bad as ever, I decided that it was either sink or swim and I knew I had to build up my self-respect as it was at rock-bottom at the time. The only thing that I knew for sure would work was to rediscover that strong young woman of 32 and return once and for all to my life-enhancing spiritual practice that I had given up when we married. It took me weeks to tell Steven about this decision.

Although he was furious initially, I made it clear that it was the only way our family would survive. I ignored all his threats and finally he relented. He was actually very supportive initially. As I became more involved, and spent more time taking part in our Buddhist peace movement, he became more disgruntled.

We both settled for some sort of compromise and life continued.

With the children grown up and away from home, on one level, things got better and there were lots of activities we enjoyed together.

I frequently felt great love for him and only occasionally contemplated leaving him.

At the same time, living with this man felt increasingly oppressive. Not that HIS behaviour was worse than normal, I was just becoming more aware of his emotionally controlling tendencies and his bullying.

I remember phoning Women's Aid, to get some information on emotional abuse and controlling behaviour. I made it clear that I did not want to leave my husband. They recommended a book to read, which I did not even order. I think I already knew the answer.

Three years before I left, a serious argument blew up and I moved out of our bedroom. This caused a lot of tension. To my great delight, Steven agreed to go to relationship counselling with me.

His behaviour during the counselling sessions was all about blaming me and I became increasingly doubtful about the wisdom of staying together.

Six months after my 65th birthday, I was asking myself, do I want to live like this for the rest of my life? To spend my time constantly endeavouring to make things better, wanting so badly to please Steven, constantly seeking his approval? Even as I write this, I can hear his arguments in my head, pointing out how badly I behaved, how unreasonable I was, how hard he tried.

The thing was, my life-force was becoming so strong that it was difficult for the same old tricks to work. My life was growing so fast that the relationship with my husband was bursting at the seams.

One phrase served as a turning point. Steven had said to me twice in anger that he "held me in contempt". One night, when he was quite calm, I asked him if he really meant that. He said quite calmly, "Oh yes, I absolutely hold you in contempt." For most women in an abusive relationship, a remark like that would probably seem quite mild compared with FAR greater abuse, but for me, it opened my eyes to the reality of his feelings for me.

That was it really…

I phoned Women's Aid again, this time saying I was thinking of leaving my husband. They invited me in for a chat. I thought they might just send me away as I was sure there were men who were MUCH worse than MY husband. To my surprise they offered me a place in a refuge.

I had a day or so to make up my mind. On the night before I left, I packed some essentials. I hardly slept that night and the next morning, I told Steven I was leaving. He said something mocking to me, but when he realised I really meant it, he started to be kind and loving. That was the hardest thing!

I reminded myself of how I had tried to leave before and then relented, being swayed by his loving behaviour which had only lasted a short time. This time I went. I packed my things, got into my car and went to live in a refuge! Waaaaaah!

I was exhilarated, terrified, sad, determined. The list of emotions is endless and I kept flitting from one to the other. Steven was devastated and this broke my heart.

He was also extremely considerate to me. Not that he tried to contact me in my refuge, but he sent flowers and loving messages through my children. That was the hardest thing, to maintain my resolve. I had WONDERFUL support from all of my grown-up children. This kept me going. The support from Women's Aid was also invaluable.

After three months, I moved into a lovely rented flat in a place of my choosing. I felt happy and safe but lonely and sad. I missed Steven and certain aspects of our life together so much. At times I wanted desperately to go back, to return to the security of the home we had shared for thirty years.

The tiniest things really got to me. I would be standing in the kitchen using a pot I had used when we were together, tears streaming down my face because I missed home so much. On the other hand, I was happy, positive and free. I have found my strong spiritual self again and that self is growing on a daily basis.

I am moving forward again!

We are now divorced and I have bought my own beautiful apartment overlooking the sea. A place where I had always wanted to live but never dared to express that desire.

My tale is not one of obvious cruelty or physical abuse. Steven's controlling behaviour was much more subtle than that. So subtle in fact that when I heard the stories of other women in the sessions I attended with an extremely supportive organisation called Saje, I felt a total fraud!

I always say it was so hard to leave, but even harder to stay away. There were so many times when I just wanted to collapse into his arms and say I wanted to try again.

So here I am at 68, living the life I want to live: I have my own small business, live in an idyllic apartment, have great friends of my choosing and wonderfully loving and supportive adult children. I could not have done this without them.

I want to finish by saying what a momentous journey I have been on and I am now truly moving forward. I have regained my spiritual and emotional well-being. I am going from strength to strength!

As a post-script I am adding some questions I asked myself for over thirty years, together with answers, not necessarily in the correctly responding order.

The purpose of this is to show how hard it was to decide to leave my marriage.

QUESTIONS WHY
- Did I not leave before I was 65?
- Did I give up a life where I was JUST beginning to blossom?
- Did I allow my husband to mistreat our children?
- Did I give up my more 'unsuitable' friends?
- Did I never speak openly about being at university, former relationships, my world travels, my eating disorder?

- Did I stop embracing a philosophy that was bringing out my greatest potential?
- Did I pretend I was happy?
- Did I not stop him from discouraging our children?
- Did I pretend I was more conservative than I really was?
- Did I silence my child about telling the hospital that it was her father who injured her shoulder?
- Did I put up with very few visitors to our house for many years.
- Did I want to keep my husband in a good mood at all costs?
- Did I feel bad when I displeased him?
- Did I allow him to knock me and my daughters to the ground when I intervened to stop his violence?
- Did I fill volumes of notebooks about my unhappiness?
- Did I not insist on us having a nice house where we could invite guests and where our children could feel comfortable and cherished?
- Did I put up with him doing all the shopping and giving me instructions of what to heat up for our meals?
- Did I not report him to the police?
- Did I not protect my children more?
- Did I not challenge his ideas?
- Did I allow him to make fun of me in public?
- Did I pretend I was happy?
- Did I allow him to make fun of my mother?
- Did I allow him to make fun of my children?
- Did I join the Catholic Church?
- Did I pretend everything was fine?
- Did I sleep in a damp bedroom for most of our marriage?
- Did I allow him to ridicule my arguments whenever I disagreed with him?

ANSWERS

- I was afraid of what people would think.
- I didn't want to "rock the boat".
- I wanted to please my husband, my parents, everyone!
- I thought others' lives were more important than my own.
- I was on a path of self-sabotage.
- I did not value my life.
- I wanted him to like me.
- I wanted him to love me.
- I wanted to impress him.
- I had traded gold for rocks.
- Leaving was an unthinkable fantasy.
- I struggled to feel anger as I had swallowed it down for so many years.
- He was very skilled at manipulating me.
- He ridiculed my ideas when I dared to disagree.
- He spoke with authority.
- I was afraid of giving the "wrong" answer.
- I thought I could make him happy.
- His needs seemed more important than mine.
- I was afraid he would stop speaking to me.
- I didn't dare to make a fuss.
- He wore me down.
- I convinced myself that things would change.
- His love was conditional.
- I thought that if I obeyed him, he would love me more.
- He was very convincing.
- I was in love with him.
- I was afraid to express my opinion.
- I was afraid he would get into trouble if I spoke out about his treatment of our children.

- I loved him.
- My parents liked him.
- He seemed to get on well with my father.
- He convinced me I was "too sensitive".
- He convinced me I didn't have a sense of humour.
- He convinced me I was impractical and a coward.

Even as I reflect on all these questions and answers, the following thoughts still trouble me.

Am I not exaggerating his faults?
How could I have left this man?
He could be so kind and generous.
He could be so supportive.
He helped my parents.
He rarely went to the pub to meet friends.
He was never unfaithful during the course of our marriage.
He believed in marriage and commitment.
He was reliable.
I found him physically attractive.

My ultimate conclusion is that no matter what his many good qualities are, I had to leave to protect my own mental health and to be a great role model for my family.

I want my experience to encourage all those who are feeling discouraged or worn down that you ARE strong.

YOU HAVE THE POTENTIAL TO BE AND TO DO WHATEVER YOU WANT!

PEACE

UNSTOPPABLE

I want people who read this chapter to know that I had a happy childhood. My parents loved me for who I was. A little overprotected but loved.

When I was a teenager I was raped by my best friend's dad. I kept this to myself until I met my first husband at the age of 18. He listened, was caring and treated me like a princess. I fell hard and deeply in love.

I became pregnant and as he was in the military we decided to get married as he was posted abroad.

The wedding wasn't really my dream wedding but I didn't care as I was marrying my prince. The day after our wedding we went on a little honeymoon. And that was the last time I saw the man I married. Our honeymoon was when he hit me for the first of many times. I overcooked his bacon and he lost it. He only ever hit me where the marks could not be seen. And straight away he was sorry and was crying and promised it would never happen again. So I forgave him.

The rest of the honeymoon flew by and before I knew it I was on my way to a new home abroad.

At first we didn't have a house phone so I couldn't phone my mum and let her know I had arrived safely. So I was abroad with no friends or family to turn to.

After we had settled he went back to work and as he left he said, 'I finish at 6, I expect you to finish unpacking and tidy up and I want pie and mash and try not to burn it.' I thought he was joking.

I started to unpack but became tired and fell asleep. I woke up to a sharp pain where he hit me in the ribs. He was yelling abuse and telling me I was useless and why had he married such a lazy fat person in the first place. And he stormed off out.

I remember sitting on the floor in the bathroom throwing up as I was so scared. I had no one to go to, nowhere to turn to. I just wanted to go home. After about an hour he came home. Knocked gently on the door and said, 'Honey are you OK? I know you've had a hard day so I went to the take away.'

I remember thinking what the fuck is he on. Doesn't he know what he just did?

I opened the door very slowly. He stood there with flowers and a take out. He took one look at me and dropped everything. He acted like nothing had happened. He was worried about the baby and me, he took me to the bedroom and made me put my feet up.

I started thinking maybe I'd made it all up. And to be honest, 24 years later, I still sometimes think this.

He was nice from then until after I had my first child. And I did think oh maybe I'd seen the last of that guy.

When my child was four months old, he got a short posting to the Falkland Islands. We came back to the UK so I could see him off. Just before he got on the plane he told me to behave myself while he was gone. And again I thought he was saying it in a jokey tone.

I stayed at my parents for a couple of weeks until one night I got a phone call from him saying that I had to go home because I was giving him a bad name by not acting like a military wife. So I went home. I got a job with the NAAFI who run the shops, pubs and clubs on the camp, just so I could have some form of adult company. I even had a girly night out where me and a friend bumped into one of my husband's work friends. He walked us to the bus stop at the end of the night. He had the hots for my friend. I thought nothing of it and went back to working, being a mum and waiting for my husband to come home.

I was quite proud of the life I had made for myself and I thought he would be too.

I was at work when he came home. I picked up our child from childcare and couldn't wait to get home. I walked through the door and for the first time and the last time he hit me in the face. He shouted how fucking dare you not be here when I get home. Who were you with and who were you sleeping with when I was away. You whore, you fucking slapper, I'll teach you for making me look bad. He beat me for what felt like hours in front of our child who was still strapped in her buggy. When he finished he told me to clean myself up and cook him his tea. I remember standing in the bathroom crying. Wondering why no one had come to help me. We lived below a military policeman. But no one came to my help. After tea he told me to put that child to bed and meet him in the bedroom. That night he raped me. The next day he went into my work personally and told them I'd tripped down the stairs and was hurt pretty bad and wouldn't be in work for a couple of days. They believed him. When I was fit to go back to work I told them what he told me to say.

I noticed over the next couple of weeks that people who I thought were my friends stopped visiting.

I found out I was pregnant again a few weeks after he got home. He went off his head and kept asking who I had been sleeping with behind his back. We hadn't slept together since that night he came home. He told me he had been told I was seen out with a man when he was away. The only man I could think of was his work colleague who was now dating the friend I had been out with that night. I tried to explain this but he wouldn't listen. That night he slept on the sofa and acted as if I wasn't there. This went on for weeks.

I became really ill while pregnant; I had to give up my job. But still I was getting the quiet treatment. I made sure he still didn't have anything to complain about. The house was spotless. His clothes were ironed the way he liked and there was always a meal on the table. But no matter what I did, I still got the silent treatment.

One night he didn't come home until late. I'd kept his dinner in the oven to keep it warm. When he came home he had been drinking. I got his meal on the table, he took one look at the plate and threw it across the room. He swore a lot and called me a stupid bitch. I don't remember how long it went on I just covered my belly and prayed it was OK.

He stormed out the house and didn't come back for a few days. I was relieved when I heard the key in the door. I felt physically sick. And again he came in like nothing had happened. When he saw that there was nothing on the table I thought he would go nuts. But I remember thinking I'd finally snap and I'd made it all up in my mind. He was glad I was resting. He took our child for a walk and came back with a Chinese takeaway.

He was nice all the rest of my pregnancy and after they were born. He was nice until he got his posting and he snapped because we were posted back to my hometown in the UK. He thought I had made it happen. I must have done something to make him get posted back there. There was no hitting involved this time but a lot of shouting at me and belittling and calling me names. This went on until the movers turned up to pack up our stuff and while my husband helped them I looked after the kids and cleaned the flat. When we were not charged for anything in the handover of the property he started to be nice.

When we got back to the UK he put on this facade of the perfect husband but by then I knew the truth. I'D MADE THE BIGGEST MISTAKE marrying this man.

I was happy to be around my friends again but slowly they stopped answering my phone calls until I only had two friends left. One even told me that my husband had propositioned a couple of my friends. And telling people lies. Then as I was unpacking boxes I came across letters from different women. Over the three years we were married, I even found a naked photo of a woman. That was the final straw. So when he was at work I packed up all his stuff into black bags, making sure I crushed up all his clothes and threw the bags out of the window. Locked and chained the doors. I phoned my mum and told her I'd thrown him out. Both my parents turned up. I showed them the letters. But I never told them what had happened to me over the years I had been married.

Once he had gone he would phone at stupid times at night and harass and swear at me. Kept telling me I was an unfit mum and he was going to make sure I'd lose the kids. He played a lot of mind games but eventually I started to get on with things.

But I was also scared to be alone and I jumped straight into another relationship. He was my protector. He took over things that I couldn't cope with which was great. And for 18 years I was happy 'ish'. He had a temper but he never hit me so I thought I had met my soulmate. He used to take the piss out of my cooking and near the end he would tell jokes in front of me to his friends. That made me uncomfortable.

It wasn't until I kicked him out for sleeping with another woman that a friend recommended speaking to Saje Scotland.

I thought she was suggesting it to help me come to terms with what had happened with my first husband and she had. But she saw something in how my second husband had been treating me. I am so glad she suggested it. I learned that he had taken a vulnerable woman and completely broken me. I can remember countless times he would lose his temper at my kids from my first marriage and at those times I was brave and stood between them. But I spent years walking on eggshells worried that the slightest thing would set him off. He would get angry if I told him the kids were driving me nuts. Or said I'd had a bad day at work. So I started to keep it to myself. He'd be furious that I'd kept secrets from him. When he got really mad he would hit walls and doors. He complained about the state of the house or what I was wearing.

He'd become quiet and moody. And when we did fight it was always me that begged him to come home after he stormed out and he never once in the years we were together said sorry. It was always me. He made me feel like I could never do anything right even down to my job. I could do no right.

I didn't see what he was doing to me until after we had separated. And even now he is using my own solicitor to play mental mind games. But thanks to Saje I now see what he's doing and most of the time I am able to cope.

I may be single now and my body is a wee bit broken, but I'm a lot wiser and unstoppable.

STAYING ALIVE

In the beginning things were good. In fact, things were fantastic... isn't that the way though?

It's not until years later and with a lot of help from many women's organisations that all the small things from the early days start to make sense.

Him going out with the buggy in the car, forgetting to leave the house key, forgetting to leave you money.

And of course, these things are complete accidents. If only I knew then what I know now.

For me, these small things turned into life-changing almost life-ending events that very quickly turned into everyday events, normality for me and my three children.

What was normal to the other kids at school was certainly not normal to my children, and what was normal to my sisters was hidden and far from normal to me.

I was a single mum of a one-year-old boy when I met my abuser. He said he loved me and my son, he acted as his father, played and supported him. I, however, slowly stopped seeing my friends as it was easier than trying to explain why I wanted to go out without him. Or if I did go out: what I had done, where I had been and most importantly who I had spoken to. Life became very isolated very quickly.

Just after a year of being together I fell pregnant. It had taken me some convincing but it was planned.

From there, his and my son's relationship changed. Suddenly my son stopped being allowed toys downstairs. His bedtime started getting earlier and earlier and fun with him completely stopped. My daughter was born and my son stopped existing. The night I arrived home after having her was the first of many nights that he raped me. I was shaking, crying and laughed at. Mocked for bleeding and not having a flat stomach anymore. Giving birth eighteen hours earlier was no excuse.

From there on things would never be the same. This is where the light from my life was switched off.

I started being the punchline to all his jokes and I was made to feel useless and unattractive, pretty much worthless.

My daughter was three months old when I fell pregnant again. I was shocked but not surprised as I wasn't allowed the pill. The conception due to me being raped again. So imagine my surprise when he went ballistic and accused me of trying to trap him. He did not want the baby and appointments were made to have a termination. Guilt!!! The final termination appointment was made for my birthday, which I kept being reminded would not be celebrated. That morning arrived and I made the decision to continue with the pregnancy, even if I was doing it alone.

Now though I had ruined his plans for drinking that night together. He drank though and decided he was going to stay. Reminding me the whole night how lucky I should feel, as plenty of women were waiting for us to split up to be with him.

The next few months were quite repetitive: rape, drinking, name calling, general unhappiness. At around five months pregnant things changed again, he started pushing me, punching, nipping, he even bit my stomach.

By the time I had given birth I had already sunk into quite a numbing depression but never to anyone else's knowledge, people would see me and think I was one of the happiest people around.

Skip forward a year, nothing had really changed except the violence was worse, the drinking was more, the combination was unbearable, so much so that heaven gained four little angels. I miscarried on separate occasions due to extreme violence such as kicks to the stomach, being thrown around the bathroom like a rag doll, my head smashed against the bath, I now have a dent in my forehead as a reminder.

He was punishing me daily.

My memories jump back and forth when I think about him. I remember him coming in from the local pub one night. He was angry he'd been thrown out of the pub for being aggressive, so straight home to make me pay. I was punched unconscious and when I came round, he was raping me and that continued for what felt like hours. The pain was so bad I kept passing out. I was bruised, cut, scratched and bitten. There was blood everywhere. I was so sore I did not have the strength in my toes to push my body up off the floor. He laughed and laughed as I crawled to the bathroom, blood running out of my bottom. My three-year-old daughter woke up to the noise, she helped clean me up thinking I was practicing for Halloween. I feel sick when I think of that night, also many others.

Sometimes I was a little braver and tried to stand up for myself, but there were always consequences. Not getting him drink on the morning school run meant a day of name calling, being nipped and my face spat on until I gave in and went to the shop for alcohol. Usually cider, beer and fags to last him until I picked the kids up again at three o'clock, then he would get more to do him the rest of the night. Not doing that was never an option as I didn't want to risk him doing anything to the kids, so it was easier to just keep him happy, which never happened either. Every time I thought I was playing his game right and was pleasing him he always seemed to change the rules, which always meant I'd done something wrong... there was no right way to do anything!!!

I tried leaving him on many occasions, I've actually lost count of how many. The main reasons for returning were guilt and empty promises. The kids would beg me to go back, they missed their dad, for the most part they did not know him as I did. The other reason was him begging for another chance and promising he wouldn't hurt me again, which makes no sense as while the violence was happening he would always say the morning after that he'd never done anything or I must have done something to make him do it. He would also promise to stop drinking. All of the above would stop for a maximum of two weeks if I was very lucky. Every time I returned all I had was hope which every time was shattered.

Even when I eventually left for good I was still his, I was branded! In his words "you are mine and always will be, nobody will want you or love you", then he would burn me with his cigarette. He would burn my breasts and bottom, so much so that in the summertime the heat and sweat cause the wounds to open up or seep. Not only does this look horrible but mentally it takes me straight back to each time they were done.

Another reminder I am left with is a haematoma on my left cheek bone, gained through another awful night. After being wakened by being dragged out of bed by my ankles again and dumped on the floor, a move I associate with wrestling, except with very real pain. He wanted sex and decided it was his right as I was his and he was horny. A few things had been knocked over in my fight to keep him off me, which woke my eldest child who came through to see me being pinned to the bedroom floor by my forehead naked with his stepdad semi naked on top of me. I begged him to go back to bed and I would come through to his room in the morning.

After my abuser finished raping me he pulled me to my feet and punched me straight to the floor, each time being punched on the cheekbone. Maybe I should have stayed down but I did not want him to think I was weak or he was stronger than me, I was filled with so much rage.

There is so much more I can say that happened over my eleven years with that animal but I don't have enough paper or time. My memories are humiliating, degrading and sickening but full of hope and strength also. I never thought I would make it out alive to be writing this but yet somehow I'm here and finally in a place where happiness exists and where choices exist. The rules I follow are of my own making and breaking. Life is not all roses but I don't have to be scared either. The scars I have go much deeper than what you can see on my body, they live with me mentally forever and I overcome them on a daily basis, from getting up and dressed, to leaving the house, to even staying alive!

My journey has taught me so much, but finally eight years on, who I am and how to be me.

NEVER GIVE UP

My children, I don't want you ever to forget how much I love you.

Sometimes parents don't make their feelings clear,
they assume that their children know of the deep love
they feel for them.

Yet, when misunderstandings occur and things are left
unsaid, it can lead to needless doubts and insecurities.

I don't ever want you to feel insecure and I want you to
remember these words I am telling you because
they are always current and never changing.

You are the greatest thing that ever happened to me.
There is nothing I'd rather see than your smile, and
nothing I'd rather hear than your laughter.

I am so proud of the person I have become and no
matter what happens in your life I have confidence and
the ability to make the right choices.

I love you.

BEING A PARENT

Somebody once told me that

Hope, Faith, Strength and Courage is all you need because being a mum you
never sit down.

You get up fight for what belongs to you

We ladies are strong, we are fighters

We never give up because we love our kids unconditionally

There are times I wish I could do better and do more

I am doing everything I can do

It doesn't matter how many courses you do, it doesn't matter what people say,
it doesn't matter what people think because

Mums are the role model in your Kid's life

As I said no matter what crap we ladies get in our life, we get up and we start
again

No matter what

We have Faith, we have Courage, we have Strength and most of all we have
Hope

Always remember, you are braver than you believe, stronger than you seem,
and smarter than you think.

Never Give Up

COURAGE

PEACE

I have thought long and hard about how to write my story, what to put in it, how to start it, how much detail do people actually want to read? I finally decided to begin with telling you how I am feeling right at this moment, and how much my life has changed.

I finally split from my partner 19 months ago. On one hand it seems like only yesterday and on the other hand it seems like a lifetime ago! My life has changed beyond all recognition. My son and I moved into our own home exactly a year ago now and we absolutely love it! The household is so calm, no stress or worry. I come home after work and actually enjoy going into the house! I have no fear about what mood he's going to be in, how his day will have gone, what will be the repercussions if I am running late or something will not be as he expected. My son has friends over whenever he pleases, more than one friend is allowed these days! My house is often full of teenagers, filling my living room as they are all well over 6 feet tall! My cupboards and fridge are often raided and it's great to see him enjoying his life with no stress or worry. He did have friends over sometimes when we lived with his father, but my son said once that he always remembers me going into his bedroom and just saying, "that's Dad home". A warning that I suppose no one else would have been aware of apart from us.

I feel like a different person these days. I have lost weight, partly due to the stress of what happened, but partly because I can go to keep fit classes and go out for runs these days, whenever I want. Life is easy these days, we do things we want to do, we can look forward to things that we've got planned because I know that I'm in control of things these days, so they go ahead with no problems or apprehension. My friends and family keep telling me I look so different. I was speaking to my best pal the other day and I was telling her that I can't put my finger on what it is, but I'm starting to remember how I used to be? I feel the old me is starting to emerge? I feel that I laugh and smile all the time these days, and I really feel that I'm laughing from the inside out! What I have found quite hard about that is acknowledging that I have been putting a front on for years and years. I still find it hard to accept that I had become such a different person. I still find it hard as I don't think I'm a stupid person and I feel that I must have been stupid to let myself lead the life I was leading. Not being myself, being so different.

It is only now that I have been out of the relationship for over a year that I can really reflect on it all, and I can see what it was like right from the beginning. I completed my course with Saje last year and it was like a revelation!! It made me see that his behaviour had been controlling and bullying right from the very start.

It was so good to speak to others who absolutely, wholly understand what you've been through. Friends and family have been great, but there is still always a feeling that people think you should have left earlier or why did you put up with that? There is always someone who says, "I would never let my husband get away with that!" and with that goes the accusation that you have been very silly to let yourself get into the situation you did.

Saje's group made everything much clearer and I finally started to see that it wasn't my fault and I wasn't stupid at all. Though that is something that I still struggle with.

My partner and I had been together for 17 years, but for that last four or five years I can now honestly say I was not really happy. I was starting to see his behaviour for what it was and was becoming very aware that it was never going to change. I can see now that as I was becoming more emotionally withdrawn from him, his behaviour was escalating. At the time I told myself he was getting worse as he was getting older, but I can now see he was just trying different tactics as his normal behaviour wasn't getting him the results he expected!

The main point of my story, the point I would like all women to realise is how extreme and how dangerous their behaviour can be at the end. If they think you are planning on leaving, if they feel their control is slipping, things can very quickly rocket out of control. As I know, to my detriment.

We hadn't been getting on for months and months and we were attending relationship counselling. We went every week and he would sit and say all the right things. I would sit and say how I felt and it's only now that I see I was not really being honest at all. I was doing my usual of saying what I thought would keep the peace!

We had a bit fall-out one Saturday night and he went out and got completely hammered. He came in around one in the morning and when he came into the bedroom I know right away I was in trouble. He was literally swaying he was so drunk. For around three hours he stood and shouted and swore at me! How everything was all my fault, I was the reason we were skint, he was stressed, he wasn't getting enough sex, I was fat, I was obviously getting sex elsewhere... all the usual stuff. He started saying 'I could punch your head in right now', 'I could fucking kill you right now'. I went to go and sleep downstairs and he grabbed me as I was getting out of bed, got my head in a head lock and bit my ear. I started screaming and he started punching me repeatedly in the head and shoulders. Our son came into the bedroom and put the light on, this gave me a chance to get out of the bed and head downstairs. I told my son to phone the police. I tried to call them myself but my partner grabbed my phone from me and smashed it up right in front of my face. I ran out of the front door, grabbing the house phone as I went and called the police. He followed me outside, me in my nightie and him in only boxers! He was shouting and swearing and grabbed the phone from me. I managed to get past him and ran back into the house, locking the front door as I went back in. He smashed his fist through the door, and I can always picture him looking at me through the hole he made in the glass. He was shouting and pointing at me saying 'this is your fault, all your fucking doing!' I actually remember thinking at that moment - bloody hell, he's actually still blaming me for all this! I also remember thinking that there was almost relief as he'd finally gone too far and I finally had a good reason to finish the relationship.

The police arrived, and he was arrested, assaulting an officer in the process!

The months that followed this were absolute hell. He would just not accept that it was over. He turned up at my work, he turned up when I was out walking the dog. He would turn up at the door, sometimes crying his eyes out... I'd broken up the family, I was upsetting our son! Then when the crying didn't work, he would get angry. He threatened to kill himself numerous times. He turned up one night, barged into the house and took the car key. He said he was going to wrap the car around a tree! We had the police at the house until the early hours of the morning until they found him. He would phone and phone continuously, leaving messages if I didn't answer. He would then start calling our son's mobile if I ignored him. In the space of five weeks I called the police five times. He cut his wrist right in front of me one day. He was bleeding all over the floor and wouldn't let me out of the door of the house. He took my hand and said 'just sit with me until it's over. I'm not living any more without you so just stay with me until it's done.'

It just went on and on and every day I woke up wondering what was going to happen that day.

Eventually he was arrested and charged with harassment and threatening behaviour and was placed under bail conditions which prevented him from contacting me or coming to my house. He continued to text me and the mistake I made was not contacting the police. It's a very difficult situation because the bail conditions meant he couldn't contact me, but all this does is make your child the messenger! It just put huge pressure on him as he became the go-between for his dad and me. It was easier to deal with my ex by myself. It made my son's life easier!

This extreme emotional behaviour continued until the final incident. As he was under bail conditions, contact with him had lessened. It was a Saturday night, my son and I were in our beds. My mobile phone rang about five times around 1am in the morning. I ignored it and turned it to silent. I knew he would be drunk and I felt that as we'd been separated for six months I didn't have to deal with his drunken ramblings any more. My son came into my room and said his dad had been phoning his mobile too so we both put our phones on silent and went back to bed. It was 3.20 am when I was woken by the sound of glass smashing. I sat up, knowing immediately that it was him. I thought to begin with he was smashing up my car, that was more his style! My son was in my bedroom within about 30 seconds, he said, 'push the button, it's Dad'. The police had given us a panic alarm due to the harassment I'd had from him. I'd really felt it was over the top! I pushed the button, but as it's a silent alarm, there is a fear that it's not working! I phoned the police from my mobile too and my son and I were at the top of the stairs. By this time, I realised that he was breaking into the house. He was smashing through the dining room window. I was speaking to the women on the phone when he appeared at the bottom of the stairs, with a baseball bat in his hand. My heart sank when I saw the bat, I realised I was in big trouble. I remember saying to the woman on the phone 'he's got a bat, he's got a bat!' Our son said, 'Dad, what're you doing?' and he just walked past me at the top step and started hitting our son, his own 14-year-old son, with the baseball bat. I was screaming, still with the phone in my hand. He was bringing the bat right back and swinging it with all his strength. My son just curled up in a ball on the ground. My boy was only wearing boxers, he thought he was too old for pyjamas! His dad hit him four or five times then turned to me. I tried to get into my bedroom and close the door but he was on me in a second, he had the bat up to take a swing at me and I remember just grabbing hold of the bat. I thought, 'If he hits me with that he'll knock me out so I need to keep hold of it.'

For what seemed like ages we basically wrestled over the bat. He was shouting and swearing at me. The usual insults... I was a slag, it was all my fault. He said I was going to die that night... and I believed him. We ended up on the ground. He was straddling me. I was still holding on to the bat and he was punching me repeatedly in the head, in my shoulder and back. At one point, when we were on the floor, I could hear a voice on the other end of my mobile phone. I must have dropped it and it had fallen somewhere near where we were. I remember thinking that the police knew what was happening and that at least they were on their way! I eventually heard them breaking my front door in. I was thinking if I could just hang on, they were coming. I was aware of my face and arms being wet so I knew I was bleeding but the bedroom was dark. At one point, he was still straddling me and his hand must have come against my thigh. My pants had got all twisted around my waist with all the fighting and he thought I had no pants on. He said to me 'you've got no knickers on, who have you been shagging tonight?' He put his fingers inside me and said, 'there you go, there you go'. Then he started shouting and hitting me around the head again. After what seemed like ages, I heard the police coming into the house. I was aware that I was starting to see stars every time he hit me and I was worried I would pass out. I was worried he would go back out to the landing and start on my son again. I wasn't sure if my son was even alive. I was sure he would be at least unconscious.

The police came into the bedroom and got hold of him. My son and I were taken to hospital in an ambulance. While we were waiting for the ambulance the police discovered where he had smashed through the window with the baseball bat. There was a knife lying on the floor in front of the window. It didn't belong to me, it must have fallen out of his pocket when he came in the window! I'm thankful for that on a daily basis! I dread to think what could have happened if he'd had that knife on him when he came up the stairs.

It was the worst night of my life but with it came the freedom that we are still experiencing. He was taken to prison that night, and has been there ever since. I have only seen him at the trial. He pleaded not guilty, so my son and I had to endure a three day trial and relive the whole thing again. He was found guilty to serious assault, not attempted murder, which I feel it should have been. He was sentenced to almost 4 years.

My son and I have since moved to a new house. We both had counselling. I had a fab counsellor through Woman's Aid, a service which has now been stopped due to budget cuts. Unfortunately, his Dad's trial came at the same time as his exams. He did very well and passed some but he is having to re-sit some of them.

I see such a change in him, he is like a different boy. We have had such freedom since his Dad was locked up. We can live our lives without looking over our shoulders. We are no longer walking on eggshells. The saddest thing for me is that I thought I was protecting him from so much but I see now that he spent his whole childhood walking on eggshells. We now go to lots of family occasions, with no stress! My son mixes with everyone, rather than sitting at his dad's side, not speaking to anyone. He is much more confident than he used to be. It's great to see him so happy and relaxed.

I completed the courses with Saje and have not long finished my training to become a volunteer. I am now supporting Saje in a range of different ways with another volunteer. It is something that is very important to me. My life has transformed in the last 18 months and I feel that if I can help one other woman in a small way it is worthwhile.

My ex's behaviour escalated very quickly at the end. He had never actually hit me before. He was someone who would smash and break things. I always knew he was capable of hitting me, but I never imagined it would end in such a violent way and I never in a million years thought he would hit his son. My son and I have had the luxury of his being locked up and it has given us the time to heal and hopefully gain strength and confidence. We have recently heard that although he was sentenced to almost four years, he will of course, only serve half of the sentence. We thought we had another 10 months of freedom but have been informed that he will very soon be moved to an open prison and will be allowed out for a week at a time, to help him reintegrate back into society! He will not be tagged and it happens to coincide with my son's exams again this year. The system is awful and certainly not victim friendly, but that is another whole book on its own!

I have spent the last year doing all sorts of things with my son and our family and friends and we have lots of things planned for the coming year. We have to focus on that and try to continue with our lives and not let the fact he is being released from prison ruin our lives. Last year we attended the Belladrum Music Festival. It is known as the Tartan Heart Festival. We were with family and had the best time ever. My son looked so happy and we laughed so much. We are already booked to go back this year!

BLUE

Blue flashing lights
Intermittent memories
Queuing to crowd my mind.
Blue sea, skies, sand and fun
Joni Mitchell - your favourite album
Your deep cold blue eyes
And me
Reflected in their azure pool
Searching, longing for signs of warmth.

Red lights flickering on monitor screens
Red curtains drawn
I hear distant voices of concern
Speaking commands
Still, I struggle to breathe
The memories cease as
Focus is imperative.
Relax. Breathe. Don't panic. I can get through this.
Blot out the memories.
Try not to remember.

But why did I trust you?
Why did I stay so long?
Broken trust, broken promises,
I fear for my child at home with him
I fear for my life.

Cardiac team at the ready
They're prepped to fix my heart
But this paper heart is torn
And things have got to change
Will change
Now blue memories dissipated
My focus turns to red.

LIVE

SHATTERED DREAMS

I have four kids, two older. I had my first at 18 and my second at 21 to a complete bad boy, a criminal in and out of jail who also did drugs. I didn't do any of that stuff and when I had my second child to him I upped and left the area when the kids were 2 years old and 6 weeks old. I moved alone with my babies. I had great support from Women's Aid. I worked on building a better life, had a few idiots along the way. I believed I had got myself over it though and ended up with a job in IT with the very organisation that had helped me.

I studied hard for my qualifications and tried to make my kids proud, until the next mistake (to cut a long story short).

I had two kids that he begged me to have. I was finished and content with my two, but he wanted his own kids. So I fell pregnant. Unfortunately, I miscarried the first child, we were devastated. He was such a good person to my kids that I just wanted to give him his own ones and we kept trying, I then fell pregnant again and he proposed we set a wedding date for after we had our baby.

I gave up my career and had our baby girl. When I was getting fitted for my wedding dress it kept getting tighter each time. Turns out I was pregnant again. Nine months between my younger two. We got married when I was five months pregnant and then I had our boy premature. It was hard and he changed into a horrible person. Horrible to my oldest two and to me. He was only interested in his own kids now. On our first wedding anniversary when we had a rare night out, he was witnessed assaulting me, by the police of all people. They took him into custody and charged him. Really, he had had me in the house for three years pregnant and under control and I stupidly wrote a letter in his favour saying what a great person and father he was. Two days before Christmas that same year he come in drunk and really in a nasty mood. I thought he was going to hit my son so I stood in front of him so I would get it instead. He then hit my 14-year-old daughter in the face. We went through courts, mediation, contact centres to keep his relationship with the two kids we had together. He was charged with the assault on my daughter and I never went near him again. It took me years to get over as I loved him. During this he met a new woman who he moved in with. Our kids were pushed to the side and their feelings hurt badly. I struggled to believe what the situation had become as he had adored his own kids and fought through all the hurdles to stay in their life, and then put this woman and her children in place of our two kids. They didn't matter anymore. I have supported the kids as best I can and they don't know we split because he hit their big sister.

Anyway, there I was, four kids (two primary school kids and two older kids) trying to heal my family with no interest in having a relationship.

Everything changed that night I walked into the local Chinese takeaway. I jokingly asked the delivery driver for a lift up the road. He said he couldn't. Then that weekend my neighbour asked me to go for a drink with her to her friend's. My eldest was home and said he would watch the kids. So I went to her friend's. When we went in they were all drunk and I didn't want anything to do with the situation. Turned out the three of them were all sleeping with the same man. I sat and had a few drinks, feeling uncomfortable, but then his cousin came in and it was the delivery guy from the Chinese takeaway! We chatted about how we didn't fit in with the situation and he told me all about himself, seemed nice enough. He asked for my number and then gave me a lift home.

As soon as I was home he was messaging. I didn't realise then but I do now: it was messages all about him and how he had had a hard life. His dad was an alcoholic and had died in his forties. He was now in his forties and scared, that's why he didn't drink and he didn't do drugs either. It all sounded good to me. He sent me pictures of his qualification from university stating he wanted me to know he was a genuine nice guy with a good career ahead of him, the deliveries job was just a gap. He had just split from his girlfriend, she had taken everything from him blah blah blah.

The next night he messaged he was outside my house. I was in my jammies and said to him he's not getting in my house. He asked me to go out so I did. My two eldest were in at the time. He took me to McDonalds in my jammies, kept complimenting me and I thought is this guy for real.

The next day the kids had school. He asked if he could take me out for the day. I said yes and gradually from there he was every day every night slowly creeping his way in. Popping by after deliveries and not wanting to go home to an empty bed, he had moved back into his mum's after he had split.

After a week of us seeing each other every day he put me on the insurance for his car as mine was sitting in the drive, broken. I now know the car was his ex girlfriend's. He had taken it off her. I didn't know this then and I drove around in it. That poor woman, she must have felt so hurt. I had no idea at the time.

Before I even knew what was happening, he was being so nice, wanting to meet my kids and my dog and my mum so I let him. He would joke and laugh with them and always be polite and happy to help them if they needed a run home. He always asked my older kids who wanted the free Chinese that he got at the end of his shift.

109

Looking back now he was just making sure they were actually leaving. My eldest son had a flat in Dundee while he was at university and my eldest daughter has her own flat.

The prick as we will call him just wanted me to himself at any opportunity. I know that now.

So I now thought what a nice guy. I had never been with a professional before. He had been to university, I had never had someone so important and educated interested in me before. He didn't drink, smoke or take drugs. I had met the one so yeah I fell head over heels in love and he loved me too he always wanted to be with me and he said his wish was to help with the kids as he didn't have any of his own.

He moved in, made it all legal. My money stopped. He got all the money but also worked off the record for the takeaway. That's when my doubts set in. The first instance was the washing machine broke down, so he bought a new one. I didn't like it being bought for me (forgetting he was getting all our money not just his, I was so stupid). He handed me £35 and asked me to fill the car for him so I went and did that. He then used it for work. We were due to leave for a holiday in England in two days which he had organised for us but had asked me to book the hotel. Another story, wait for it.

He got in from work and he had steam coming out his ears. *I did not put the whole £35 in the car, how dare I lie, what did I do with the money.* I was gobsmacked and he ranted at me for hours about going to check the CCTV at the garage and I might as well admit I had not put the money in the car. The kids were in bed but my eldest and his girlfriend were in. My son tried to get involved but I said it was fine and asked the prick to leave. The kids had woken up. He said he

110

would be back for his washing machine and I wasn't getting money or the car until I told the truth. He left.

I had just got back from walking the kids to school. They had been upset asking where the car was and what the shouting was about. They'd had so much hurt in their wee lives and they were all set for going on holiday. How was I going to tell them we weren't going? I arrived home and he was already at the door. He said sorry it was his mistake, the garage I'd used was known for the fuel not being correct measures. I felt at that moment I had to give in for my kids, but I had now seen him in a very different light.

We went on holiday and he wasn't happy with the hotel I had booked. He chose everything we did and I then found out he had taken his ex and her kids there loads. He also was calling her and demanding possessions and money off her when we were down there with him… poor woman, I had no idea. Our holiday consisted of him choosing our day activity and then at night the town was no place for kids so we sat in the rooms. I started not to like him very much.

When we got back (he had only been moved in about a month by then), he decided he wanted to decorate our bedroom and the upstairs bathroom. Went away and got on with it. At the time I thought why not the living room or why the bedroom… yeah it was because that was where he was going to live, in the bedroom, while giving me the silent treatment, and the upstairs bathroom was his - we were to have the downstairs one. He also bought roller blinds for every window in the house as he liked our privacy. The blinds were to stay shut as there were work men building houses over the road from us.

My uncle died and my aunt gave me a caravan. I parked it round in my oldest daughter's garden. The prick decided we would buy a new second car that would be his and he could then tow the caravan for holidays. And all he kept saying to the wee kids was *your mum needs to agree to marry me it would be so good we could be a family* etc. All these happy things but I knew I would never marry again so I kept reassuring the kids we didn't need that.

Mother's Day was coming up and my eldest was organising a meal for me. The day before, my youngest daughter had a party. I forgot to say, it turns out my two kids were in his niece's class at school; they had become good friends and we had her often. We had her that day so the girls were at the party and my wee boy was playing at a friend's. Once the party was over, I dropped the girls off with the prick and headed up to get my boy. I had a cuppa there with the mum, said thank you and came home. The prick was actually foaming at the mouth, steam coming out the ears. His niece was due home at 5.30. I arrived home at 5.25. I suggested he could nip her up and he went off on a big rant so I took her home. I came home to fireworks - he wanted to take both my kids to get me a Mother's Day present but as I had arrived back late it was now impossible for him to take them to the shops, they were all closed, how dare I decide to stay for a cup of tea with my boy's friend's mum (my oldest kids had organised Mother's Day for me with the wee kids, he knew that). Anyway, I got the silent treatment as he wanted to be involved on Mother's Day and he was being pushed out. I was informed that if I went for lunch with my kids he expected me to be home for four so he could have half an hour with me before he went to work. He had me 24/7!!!

I went for lunch and didn't come back for four. I think it was three days before he spoke to me again, he just sat upstairs in the room, the kids were confused and kept asking what was wrong with him.

His mum had a heart attack a couple of days later. He didn't take time off work to go see her, so I went up to visit, took chocolates and

112

magazines. I hardly knew the woman but I felt so bad she was in hospital with no visitors that day. When I arrived in her room the prick called me and I answered but felt quite rude talking on the phone while visiting so I just agreed and didn't listen to what he was saying. Once I was out the hospital I popped to ASDAs for a few bits and he called me again. *Well where was I*, he asked. I said ASDAs. He said *no you told me you have been to ASDAs then the hospital so why are you lying and I can hear you're walking, I can hear the wind, you're not at ASDAs at all.* I had been to Sainsburys before the hospital but I actually took my receipts home to show him.

God, the next argument came in the form of: my eldest had a dog she couldn't cope with, so we were trying to find it a home. My friend's ex who she is still good friends with, offered to meet the dog and see how it went. None of them drove so I said I would pop the dog up. I invited the prick and I took my younger kids with me. The prick said he wasn't going. When I got home, he said I had been away with this man walking the dog doing all sorts and he was ranting about it all. I actually got to the point I just kept quiet. There was no point trying to even explain I had my kids and myself, my friend and her kid were there with her ex who is still a friend.

Another time I popped to ASDA with the kids, forgot something and went into the Aldi I was passing to pick it up. I was reminded I should text if my plans change i.e. if I go to ASDA, text, then Aldi. I should text as he could see my Facebook was active at all times so I was obviously on Facebook not in the shops for that long. I started logging out of Facebook so I couldn't get accused of hiding things and always being online.

He had by then got me a contract mobile in his name. He paid the bills. This was obviously to keep checks on me, but at the time he made out he was helping me: he would pay the bill and I would have an up-to-date mobile phone.

Every time there was an important day for the kids or myself, I worked out he would kick off, sulk and then make a big gesture. The next gesture was after I put petrol in the car once again. I was cautious as I knew what he was like, so I had a receipt. He went to work and then called me: I must have put diesel in the car as it was kangarooing. I actually called the garage to check with the woman. She remembered me and we both knew I had put the correct petrol in. I was second guessing everything I did by then. When he come home he said sorry.

He wanted a night away so we sat and arranged a hotel which I was to book. He looked it over and said yes and I booked the Enchanted Forest for us to visit, it would be good for the kids. But Nah he hated the hotel and hated the Enchanted Forest, made it very clear to the kids and they were so enjoying it.

He was even more peculiar when we got home. Now I was to drop the kids at the school and go sit in the bedroom while he slept as he needed to feel me next to him or he couldn't sleep. He worked nights at the deliveries and slept during the day. He started trying to pay my elder kids to babysit their siblings so I could go deliver with him most nights. I began to refuse and he would ignore me for days or come in with a new thing I had done wrong that day. If he came in and I wasn't in bed waiting for him he would go upstairs and text me abuse about why I wasn't in bed. Even if I had my older kids over to visit for a catch up, he would say how I was neglecting him and should be going to bed.

For Christmas I wanted the kids' room done. That was most important for me. I wanted new beds for their Christmas gift and he

114

wanted a TV put in their room... I allowed it but I didn't want a TV in their room or ours; I enjoyed spending family nights round the TV in the living room. The day before Christmas he came in from work and I said, 'Oh what a boy' – a bit of a joke, as my son had nearly killed the fish (he'd tried to take it out the basin while I cleaned the tank)... But the prick said *well he should be made to watch everyone open their presents and he should get none of his till Boxing Day for his cruelty.* We argued and I told home to leave. He didn't, he did silent treatment for days.

I had had enough. The rules kept changing and I never knew what they were. My kids were living in a silent zone or a war zone. Every time I managed to get rid of him he would take the money, take the car and my mobile phone off me... and rant at me until I was brainwashed into or just suppressed into agreeing to having him back.

The last straw - I ended up going nowhere, the kids went nowhere, we were conditioned in a manipulative way for an easy life to sit in the house while he sat upstairs. May I add, in the first six months he would be nice and offer me a long lie while he would get up, give the kids breakfast and watch cartoons with them. This was a ploy to use against me later. If I got up during the night for a drink or when I came downstairs in the morning, he had told me to wear a house coat as you never know who could see in the little spaces at the side of the blinds. It was just mental and getting worse.

It got to the point where he would start an argument that was so out there and bizarre that I got angry and screamed. This was after hours of him ranting at me about all these things I had supposedly done to be convinced I was the crazy one. I just used to scream *get out go away I don't want you here.*

115

I felt horrible for my wee kids seeing silent treatment and hearing arguments when they were in bed. I just wanted an out. I knew it wouldn't be an easy one but I never imagined what came next.

It was a Saturday. My son wanted Pokémon cards, everyone had them, so I took the kids down the local high-street in the hunt for Pokémon cards. There were none so we nipped to the next town's ASDA where we got some. When we got home the prick was on silent treatment. I had messages that I hadn't noticed which stated how much he needed me that day, it was his dad's birthday and he was upset and I wasn't there for him. I came in, made the dinner and he walked straight past the dinner and put himself on a bit of toast. My switch of one whole year of this just flipped. All for the sake of some bloody cards and I was going to get silent treatment or ranted at until I agreed with him I had done wrong.

The kids were in and he wasn't for leaving. I politely said get out there's a bag, pack it and collect your belongings when the kids are at school, I don't want them seeing this. He went up down up down storming around the house ripping clothes out of drawers and cupboards, smashes and crashes. Well, my eldest daughter came in and the kids were distraught, saying the prick had been bad again. When he's like that he had agreed with the kids he should go back to his mum's until he feels better and wants to sort the problem out. He had refused. My little boy had actually tried to kick him in the middle saying don't you touch my mum. My eldest daughter is a strong girl after my ex-husband and she said *mum he's not leaving he wants to torment you and the kids so you go, I will let you know when he's gone.* He wanted the money out my purse and the sim and the phone that had my life on it. I gave him it all. Later, I found out he cut the land line cable and took the router. He took the car back, the red one he had for me. I expected that even though he had another car. I left, went for a walk. I was determined this time was it. I thought long and hard and made my mind up. No more. I knew my daughter would keep my kids safe while I wasn't there, and he knew my daughter and the situation with my ex as I had told him my life story. So I knew he would leave with his tail between his legs and not cause trouble with her.

I come home so relieved but the red car was still in the drive. He had the keys, so I knew he would be back at some point for it. We went to stay with my daughter at her flat. He came chapping the windows but she threatened him with the police and he left.

Monday morning I had all his stuff packed for him. On my way back from the school he was waiting at the bottom of the hill and followed me. I got in the house and he put his foot in the door. I shouted *everything is outside you are not getting in* and pushed him back while I locked the door. Knowing a personal family situation concerning my eldest daughter, that had nothing to do with my two younger children who weren't even alive at the time, the prick then screamed to all the neighbours *that woman is a paedophile lover, don't let your kids play with hers as there's no telling what they might do and I will be telling my sister in law the same,* (my daughter was best friends with his niece). For the record, my eldest daughter was abused as a child by my mother's husband, not my father, her new husband. I was devastated he had not only come out with this but twisted it to me and then on to my wee kids. EVIL. He was screaming he had paid for everything, it was all his, he wanted the kids' beds back, their TV, no way, they were gifts from Santa...

Everything went quiet until we arrived back from school that afternoon. He parked our red car that the kids thought was ours at my next door neighbour's. He offered to take her kid to school every day and pick him up every night (he is at school with my kids) and then went on to tell her and her big-around-town mate how I laugh at

117

them and talk about them all the time. She told me. He was emailing me by now as I didn't have a phone anymore and had to borrow a router for the internet as he had that too. He was emailing me he was welcome to take her boy to school and go sit in her garden with her any time, by then he was driving up and down past the house. I got a taxi to my eldest daughter's, left the wee ones there and went to the police.

When I went into the police station, said I wanted advice, gave my name, the lady behind the desk said *we have had him in, he is livid, shouting about beds, I think you need to speak to someone*. So I did. I explained and asked them to tell him to stay away. I had given him the two cars and he had all the money that was worth more than two beds and bedroom furniture. The police said they were going to have a word.

That night I got endless emails pages long about how I hadn't been there for him when he needed me the most, I was too busy with my kids, and if I reconsidered and changed I would get the car back and any money I needed. Next day I went to the job centre to try sort money out. He must have thought I was going to tell them about his sneaky job at the Chinese and he followed me in, said in front of the security, *I know where you live*. I went back to the police who said they would have another word. He then came to my door. I called to report it.

During all this and the upset, my wee daughter told me the niece was no longer allowed to talk to them. I went to the mum and tried to explain, but no, my kids had lost their good wee friend because of the prick telling horrible stories. I was still getting emails to watch my back as he had told all the 'big' names he knew had that I had been talking about them in a bad way. I then carried a panic alarm and had anxiety really bad. I also got an appointment with a lawyer.

118

Luckily - and I thank God for this – the prick was also messaging my oldest daughter, telling her to get me under control and to make me see sense. He would then give me money and the car, he wouldn't need the beds and the furniture, it would all be okay and we would all be happy together again.

The lawyer I saw got this information but he was dismissive saying *it will all calm down*.

I went to collect the kids from school and the police turned up to arrest me. I tried to get the kids out of the way and said could they please come back when I had organised care for my kids. Now the prick had also emailed me he was going to report me to social work telling them I don't get up with my kids, they climb around worktops looking in cupboards for food that isn't there, they are starved and I drink all the time.

Anyway, I thought yeah he will say I've scratched his car or something stupid...

No. I was arrested for assault, they took me in, booked me, searched me. My eldest daughter came with me. I called the lawyer and he said *say nothing, I will be there right away*.

I have never in my life been in trouble, never been inside a police building past reception. The scariest event of my life. I adore my daughter. Before they could go any further, she said to the Sergeant, *I have emails from him threatening to do this if mum didn't take him back*. There it was in black and white thanks to my superstar. I was interviewed and said no comment, then they let me go. It was like a dream.

I think he knew then Game Over, I wasn't going back to him, my poor kids had lost friends and I could not walk the streets for fear of randoms attacking me because of his lies. He had all the cars so I had to walk to and from school but I had informed the school of the situation. On top of it all, the caravan we never got to use - he reported my daughter for having it in her garden and the council told her to move it. I couldn't as I didn't have a car, so I sold it. But that was the beginning of the climb back up from being on my knees once again because of a man. I contacted social work after my arrest scenario to let them know of my situation.

From there the recovery began. I was put in touch with Saje Scotland and other organisations. One worked with me and the kids doing a course about types of domestic abuse. I then went on to do the Tool Kit and the Mark Brown project.

I am a very different person. I still got emails up til six months ago but I stopped reading them. It was all about him and what I had did to him and how dare I even think of having another man in my bed I'm disgusting blah blah. Within five months of us splitting after a year together, he managed to get some poor woman to marry him. She is driving around in the red car and they go on holiday to that same English town often ha-ha. But she has two poor kids the same ages with mine. I hate to imagine her life, but I do not let myself.

I finally am free - no anxiety, I support my kids best I can, content I'm a single mum, no dads in contact, I am enough. I choose to not want a man. I'm back at college studying my HND in Networking, similar to the career path I was supposed have many years ago before the husband and then the prick held my life up. I also hold down a job in a call centre to make ends meet. My kids don't go without and are the kindest, most understanding little people in my world. I'm proud to say no man just me and the kids do just fine. Saje helped me find myself again and I now know the signs of a perpetrator. I wish I found Saje twenty years ago. Or do I? I really believe it has been how it was meant to be, the lessons I've learned, the games men play and the rules changing - I honestly had no idea.

I have come to the conclusion I prefer that friend you can turn to when you're in need of no strings, no complications and I'm not ashamed of it, it is a choice I make in life and none of anyone's business. Let them judge let them gossip I don't care. The ex-husband was a violent dick and the next was a prick. I had never heard of gaslighting or the narcissist but yeah I know all the warning signs now. For my sins all my kids have been affected but it has made them better people, my kids are understanding but not stupid, never as stupid as I was. Also I never valued myself. I have allowed men and friends and family to treat me badly. I only ever stood up to them if they did anything to upset my kids. This has all changed. I value myself as well thanks to Saje and their courses.

My last pursuer was better the devil you know than the devil you don't. Someone I knew when I was younger got back in contact, he seemed like Mr Nice and I thought I know this guy so it's good. No! He decided I was a soft mum who let my kids away with too much and I couldn't drive well and I was a lousy cook. All within a month.

This time I got rid but not before putting him straight - he wasn't a parent, didn't have kids and he didn't have a driving licence and couldn't cook, so I said I am a good mum, driver and cook.
And then I said goodbye.

BREATHE

FEELING BRAND NEW WITHOUT YOU

You've got my money in your pocket like a secret affair.
You like hanging out in bedrooms like you don't even care.

You keep tampering with fire alarms, tampering with fear.
You know I hate you now, but the feeling hate - it ain't even near.

I see the evil in your eyes and you neglected my heart.
It was like I was a dart board - you kept throwing the darts.

I forgive you to forget
cause you gave me the courage to control the regret.

I have changed dramatically where you just stayed the same.
I ain't gonna name names but you should feel ashamed.

Gonna end this on a positive so thanks for the strength.
All I'm gonna do now is trust the best with length.

I show smiles yet there is only pain beneath. I write about it all the time, in my mind and in my heart it's sealed, my heart needs to be healed, it's going down field. Fearing it gets weak and loses its protective shield. All those hateful words you say all the physical violence, each time I repeat them in my mind they get slower. I once looked for the warmth on your shoulder, I felt it - feels much colder. I know when I must walk my own way - so I let you go.

THOUGHTS

Unwelcomed existential dread.

Residing on some middle ground.

The function of music is to release us from the tyranny of conscious thought.

Constant deterioration and malfunction of the human race.

A world evidently devoid of so many people who have a working conscience of the capacity to love.

Problematic, systematic, overfilled with emotions, subsiding, overflowing, mellow dramatic, stand up, room spinning, lights dimming, imagination creating worse scenario, fainting, reminiscing floating pictures blurred vision in the kitchen stacking peppers on a mission rhyming instead of singing how I feel or how I felt when feelings went missing.

Do not change your nature simply because someone harms you.

Do not lose your essence only take precautions.

JIGSAW

Slowly as I walked up the stairs the fear and panic set in, this was a different fear than I had experienced in the past. This was like entering a forest of the unknown and not knowing where it was going to take me. The forest I call counselling. Due to domestic abuse I experienced in the past I had been referred for trauma counselling.

As the counsellor introduced herself, I felt very anxious as I found it hard to trust others. Now I was having to put my trust into a complete stranger who was going to help me deal with events I had buried deep inside, events I had not addressed. Events which after 20 years were finally catching up with me like a train crash, the back end of the train having finally caught up with front. Many thoughts and emotions were running through my body. Could I handle reliving the past, would I be believed, could I mentally and physically cope with opening up properly for the first time. Only time would tell if I could.

As I sat in the room, she explained to me how the treatment was going to commence: at all times "I" was in control of how much I wanted to open up. I found this hard as I never felt during my marriage I had been in any kind of control. It was quite scary. I was continually made aware I was in a safe environment.

The first session consisted of giving my counsellor a background as to why I had ended up sitting across from her.

Throughout my journey I am referring to my ex as the COWARD. There are many other words I could use but coward seems appropriate for someone who physically and mentally abuses a woman.

As my session continued, I explained a bit about the background. Before I met the coward I was a happy girl, young, content with life. I had just commenced a career within the civil service. I loved to be with family and friends. I used to love making others smile. I was with the coward for about 13 years before we separated. I had a very happy childhood.

In the beginning the coward was charming, funny, good looking, life was full of fun. He was respectful, showering me with affection. However slowly the coward's mask started to slip. One by one the lovely things I saw slowly disappeared. I had been 17 years old when we met in a nightclub through mutual friends. We were together for 4 years before we got married.

Just before we got married he joined H M Forces. I fully supported him in his decision. As he had informed the forces he was in a long term relationship I was called upon to also be interviewed by H M Forces to see whether I was suitable to be a forces wife. If I had failed the interview he would not have been able to join up. I attended an interview where I was grilled. How independent was I? Would I conform to their rules? How would I react if we were married one day and he was posted abroad the next? I was very independent, had my own career so I would be fine. I have often asked myself if this was the start of the control.

The coward left a couple of months later for training. As I waved him off on his journey I was sad but also happy as he was doing something he wanted to. It was three weeks later before he made any contact with home. This should have been an alarm bell to me but the alarm failed to go off. After his training he had a passing out parade which I attended. I was not able to call home as I was not given the opportunity to ring my parents. It became all about his family.

We eventually got married. The coward had received his first posting miles away from home. We were allocated our first home. I went down with the coward for a couple of days to move furniture in and returned home as I was waiting a transfer with my work.

As I waved goodbye to my family and friends my new adventure of a forces wife was about to start. I had a mixture of emotions, sad to leave my parents and family and friends but also excited to see my new home, my first ever home with my husband.

The journey took about 12 hours, arriving at nearly midnight. I was cold, tired, knowing we still had to empty the van. As I looked at a block of run-down flats in front of me I burst into tears, the reality of me being so far away from home, family, friends had set in. I pulled myself together and a few days later I returned home awaiting my transfer. I received a transfer about 2 months later. I set off once again for my "marital home" but this time there was no coming home. I did not know how long this would be for. I became more anxious as I was starting in a new office not knowing anyone.

When I entered my new home, I could not believe the state it was in. It was filthy, smelly, the carpet could not be seen for clothes lying everywhere. As I walked into the kitchen there in front of me was a large box overflowing with rubbish, empty bottles of wine shoved into the fridge. I had no words. The coward had been living in the house for 2 months and had not lifted a hand to clean up his mess. The sink was covered in dishes. What had I done? Who was he expecting to clean the mess that he and his friends made?

At this point he told me he had been late for work and as a punishment he had to do extra duties after work every night for seven days. He would be out the house from 8am until 10pm for the next seven days. I felt completely let down and alone. I spent the next week feeling like Cinderella trying to make our home lovely.

I came across an open case in the bedroom. It was full of photographs and letters from other women. These women had been writing to the coward for months. I read the letters which were full of sexual communication to my husband. Letters from women looking forward to seeing him. What the fuck was he doing when I was at my parents? Why were they writing to him? I sat on the floor in tears not knowing who the man was that I married. I confronted him and he said these women had just wanted pen pals from the forces. What, pen pals who wanted sex? I was in total shock. I felt numb. This was the beginning of my journey into hell. The part of my life where all the jigsaw pieces were scrambled. He continued to blame others for getting these women to write to him.

The following week I commenced work. However, on the second day 20 miles away from home my car broke down. I contacted the coward who basically left me to deal with the breakdown myself. I was left alone in a place I did not know. I did however cope with it myself with no help from the coward.

I tried to settle into forces life. I slowly met new friends, one of whom became my rock over time at this base.

As I started to relax in the counselling, the counsellor took my journey back to various incidents over the years in a safe controlled environment. As I visualised a safe place in my mind's eye, I felt the sun beating down. I felt so peaceful, smelling all the smells around me when all of a sudden, Bang: a flashback. The counsellor was aware this was happening and asked me to tell her what was happening.

I am with the coward and family members, we have been out, we are walking home holding hands, laughing, and talking. It has been a good night. One of our friends was staying over so the coward had given him a key to let himself in. As we approached the house the door was open and keys in the lock. We went in. Our friend said he was going to be sick so I got a basin of water so he could be sick into it. He knocked the basin, spilling the water. The coward told me to go to bed and he would join me once our friend fell asleep.

I went to bed and woke up to find the coward not in bed. I got up and went to the living room, saying are you coming to bed? He jumped out of the chair. I continued back to the bedroom aware he was coming to bed behind me. I turned around to speak to him when all of a sudden I felt myself being thrown backwards onto the bed, an overwhelming pain soared across my face. What had just happened?

Realisation suddenly dawned on me. I had been hit. I ran to the bathroom, looked in the mirror. My eye was completely closed, swollen, bruising appearing all over my face. The coward ran out of the house. I immediately went to get help from the coward's sister and brother-in-law who were on holiday at ours. My then brother-in-law went out to look for him but could not find him. I went to bed in pain, shocked, scared, confused, shaking, what had I done to deserve that? Nothing, absolutely nothing. The next day I went to the hospital. His sister came with us as I did not want to be alone with him. The triage nurse at the A&E wrote down "assaulted by husband" to which he replied *I did not assault her*. His sister said you did because you hit her, that's assault.

Sitting in the waiting area I could feel all the stares from the other people waiting. The room became eerily quiet with everyone glancing out of their eyes in my direction. I felt totally embarrassed, humiliated and petrified. I was called for an X-ray then seen by a doctor. The doctor told me that I had broken bones in the orbital area. He said I had been punched. The medical term used was orbital blowout. I told him I had been slapped not punched but the injury indicated a full-blown punch. I was taken to a cubicle where a nurse tried to persuade me to report this to the police. However, as the coward had been working on me making me feel sorry for him, I refused, claiming it had been an accident. Little did I know this was just the beginning of what was to come. The coward continually used mind games to make me think he had changed, he would never do anything again.

The coward started to be nice, offering to help me round the house but this became short lived when the next incident took place. He came home one evening having been drinking. He became aggressive. The next thing he took out a penknife and thrust it in my face. Terror succumbed me, I ran for the phone. At this point he fled. I phoned my friend hysterically and she came round immediately, it was about 2 or 3 am. She sat with me when the coward returned, laughing and joking with my friend as if nothing had happened. He was like Jekyll and Hyde. Once again I received promises this would not happen again. He was sorry. The pattern commenced again helping around the house, being nice to me.

It was not long before he sat me down wishing to start a family. He knew I wanted a family so everything that had happened went out of my head. I fell pregnant but sadly miscarried. I was devastated. I miscarried on 23rd December, yet on Christmas Day having cooked a meal for him and his friend, I found myself alone as the two of them went to the pub. Here I was again feeling like Cinderella.

I pushed myself into work then found out I was pregnant again. I gave birth to my first child who became my focus. Everything seemed fine however slowly the other side of the coward started to appear. He would start going out for nights out and failing to return home until the following morning or the next evening. My mind went into overdrive. Had he been in an accident? Was he with another woman? Each time it was the same excuse: he had fallen asleep at his friend's and lost track of time.

In reality he was having an affair, an affair he had started when I was living with my parents before we were married, an affair which lasted until my oldest was nearly two. My suspicion had been right. My mind was spinning. I had the chance to leave but I didn't. *Why*, I ask myself? Well he had chipped and chipped away at me for years. I had little confidence. I did not feel strong enough to take that step. I also worried the H M Forces would intervene and allow my child to be left with the coward, as I would have no home. This was happening to others. I was emotionally broken.

One evening I had put my son to bed. The coward was out again drinking. I was in my bedroom when he came home drunk shouting he was going to take my son and I would never see him again. This time I did call the police. As I was living in married quarters I was on MOD property and therefore both civilian and MOD police turned up. When the coward knew I had phoned the police he pulled the phone cable. I thought he was going to strangle me with it so I ran out of the house to neighbours. The police went into the house, I was told by the officers that they were trying to get him out of the house so he could be arrested for breach of the peace but they could not prise my son off him as he had hold of him. Another neighbour went into the house to take my son. We stayed at her home that night.

The next day the coward came home to tell me he had been posted. No one in the police helped me that night as civilian police passed it over to military and they did not do anything. As far as they were concerned the coward had not committed a crime, had only threatened me. I felt very let down as the MOD failed to recognise what was going on behind closed doors of forces married quarters.

We moved to our new base, here I go again making new friends, awaiting transfer with my work. I had a car accident, was taken to hospital but instead of the coward supporting me he went mental at me as now we had no car, we had to borrow one from a friend. He never asked if I was OK, just kept chipping at me how we had no car and it was my fault.

I soon fell pregnant with my second child. At the birth, the coward kept leaving the room. Unknown to me at this point he was having another affair. As I was in labour he was leaving the room to phone his mistress. I gave birth to a girl, he called her his little princess however within 6 months of her birth I had to go into hospital for an operation. He came to visit. The ward was full of other patients and their visitors. It was here the coward chose to disclose he was having another affair and wanted a separation. Crying, I ran out of the ward. The ward sister was so concerned about me she called my parents who were looking after my children. It was now I had the strength to contact a solicitor, not for legal separation but divorce. I contacted a lawyer to commence legal divorce proceedings. The coward was shocked. He said he thought I was just going for legal separation. I had had enough now. Divorce it was.

Emotions of fear, insecurity, loneliness, exhaustion and panic set in, where was I going to go. I applied for a council house. The coward told me he would allow me to stay in the quarter until I found somewhere else. However, this was a lie. He immediately booked

132

himself into single accommodation on the base and as a result the forces turned up on my door and served me with an eviction order to vacate the property within 92 days. They made it clear under no uncertain terms I was no longer a part of the forces community. I had done nothing wrong yet myself and children were made homeless. I was suffering from post-natal depression at the time, I could not cope but I found the strength to get through every day. My family and friends were a great support. I started to think all the abuse would be over, how wrong was I. Not only was I being harassed by the coward but also by his mistress and the forces themselves. The forces continued to increase my rent, failed to provide me with adequate support, failed my children in favour of the coward who was a serving member of the forces. He was one of them so he had the protection, he had a roof over his head, food in his stomach, he had his career. My life left in tatters, my children and I homeless, struggling financially, worrying what road of my life was I about to embark on. My GP intervened with the forces as I was very ill and did not need the additional pressure of them also harassing me to vacate the property. When a family enters or leaves the property the forces carry out what is called a march in and out, this is basically where the property is fully inspected for faults, dust, marks on carpets, walls or any damage. Once I had the keys to my own home I was told I had to complete this "march out". However, having been told previously I was no longer anything to do with the forces, I refused to do it, advising them I was a civilian and not anything to do with the forces like I was told.

I moved into my own home with my children. It felt so peaceful and safe. Finally I was free from the mind manipulation, free from abuse free to make my own choices. I gradually built up my friends some of whom had stopped visiting me due to the coward's behaviour and attitudes in front of them. He would belittle me and be rude to not only my friends but my family. Life as a single parent was difficult. I was diagnosed with panic disorder, taking panic attacks. I was scared to leave the house.

Before I moved into my new home the coward threatened to take my children out of school and running the car off the road. I received harassing calls from him and his mistress calling me a psycho bitch, unfit mother, useless, drunkard. They had both been phoning me. I called the police but yet again as he was serving in the forces the civilian police passed it over to the forces police. This was not followed up with me so have no idea if it was taken seriously or not.

Flashback after flashback engulfed my mind. My son crying at the top of the stairs, I went to comfort him, I was half way up the stairs when the coward grabbed me and pushed past me as I lost my balance. He was screaming "he has got to fucking learn". Terrified he was going to harm him I pleaded to see to my son. My son had been referred to a consultant due to toilet accidents he had, this was all put down to stress.

My daughter was also referred for counselling as she had started to self-harm, this was all put down to the fact her father did not want to see her or bond with her. He had access every second weekend and half the school holidays yet failed to honour this. In the beginning he would take both the children. However, my youngest would become distressed and did not want to go, so in the end my son went alone. This was short lived as the coward could not have them one weekend due to illness. He never came back for them after that.

His relationship with his mistress ended, she called me to apologise! I had tried to warn her what he was like yet he had manipulated her head, and she had believed him until his true colours appeared to her. She had a child with him when we were still married, the child was taken into care after the coward refused custody of him. The coward was now in yet another relationship, again I tried to warn her but again I was not to be believed until yes you got it, the same happened to her. Now she knew the truth, the truth I had been saying all along. My youngest was curious about what the coward was like, what he looked like. So when she was 15 years old, they met up. She returned home asking me why I had married him as he was ugly. She said *I mean ugly in the inside*. She had seen him for who he is.

Over the years I suffered physical, emotional, financial abuse and am slowly getting my head around the fact that there was also sexual abuse. He had slowly over time chipped away at me until I was broken, until I was no longer any use to him, when there was nothing else to break, this was when he moved on to his next victim.

I was referred by a friend to contact Saje as I had got remarried but I was pushing my husband away. I had no idea what I was doing, I flinched when he came over to kiss me. I couldn't sleep if he was not in bed beside me. I was jumpy in the car. I phoned Saje who were brilliant, I was listened to, not judged and I was believed. I was enrolled on one of Saje's programmes, which has changed my life. Each week we listened to various topics on abuse. I was so shocked to realise I had actually suffered more abuse than what I initially thought. Speaking with others who knew what it was like was so refreshing. As a result of the programme I referred myself to Fife Rape and Sexual Assault Centre who suggested I may be suffering from PTSD - post traumatic stress disorder. I contacted my GP and was referred to a psychiatrist who confirmed in fact I did have PTSD. I started seeing the psychiatrist hand in hand with Women's Aid counselling and slowly I started coming to terms with all the abuse I had been through. I began to realise pushing my husband away was my subconscious recognising the dangers of the past and not being in the here and now.

Piece by piece I have been fitting the jigsaw puzzle of my life together and for the first time I can understand why I have been getting triggered in certain situations. Why I could not sleep if my husband was not in the bed. I still have a few pieces to join up but I know I am in a safe, happy environment now.

The abuse led to me having to give up my career, losing my sense of direction, emotional trauma, physical pain, panic attacks, PTSD, depression, failure to trust others, losing my confidence, being made homeless with two children yet through it all I am here, here stronger than ever.

Today I am happily married to a man who treats me with respect, is loyal, trustworthy, treats me as an equal, helps with the chores, loves me, makes me feel safe, regards my children as his own, treats them like his own children.

Both my children have had their own personal journeys attached to domestic abuse with my son also having PTSD, but for an unfit mother I did OK having put my son through university, supported my children, put a roof over their head, fed them with no help from the coward. They are both incredible despite the rollercoaster of a journey we have had. Both having successfully secured employment. They are a credit to me and their stepfather, a man who deserves the title of dad. He has been so supportive in my journey recovering the jigsaw pieces. One of the main issues I struggle with is being in a car due to the coward driving too fast and threatening to run the car of the road. My husband is trying to give me new memories to overcome this.

It has been a long bumpy ride but I can see through the trees now. One day the coward will have the karma bus stop at his station, there will be a few seats he can choose from. During my journey a wise lady once said to me "and this too shall pass", a phrase I continually use as sure enough it does pass. The storm may be raining heavy but the sun shines brighter.

As they say everything happens for a reason. My reason is to tell my story, allow voices to be heard which were ignored. To show others life is definitely greener on the other side, and "true love" does definitely exist. Believe in yourself! ♥

HIDDEN

Having been diagnosed with Post Traumatic Stress Disorder (PTSD) I have been trying to make sense of the years of emotional abuse I suffered. I was originally diagnosed with panic disorder. However, after having a session with rape crisis centre it became apparent that my symptoms were actually PTSD. I contacted my GP who referred me to a psychologist where I received the diagnosis of PTSD with associated panic attacks.

I received counselling from Women's Aid and it was during these sessions that I came to realise over the years that my own daughter had been a significant trigger in my life. Not through any fault of her own but because she looks like her father who had carried out years of abuse towards myself and my eldest child. This realisation was one of the hardest parts of my journey. Subconsciously my brain had been putting me on high alert whenever my daughter had a tantrum, typical of any child. However, rather than putting boundaries in place like I had with my other child, I found myself giving in to her to save the peace. I feared her subconsciously, but until I attended the counselling I had not been aware of how much the emotional abuse had impacted on our family life. Unknown to me, I had actually been scared of my own daughter through no fault of hers or mine. The fact that she reminded me of her father on a daily basis subconsciously filled me with fear, and as a result I allowed her to get away with things I would not let my eldest away with.

The self realisation of this part of my journey caused me to realise just how much control my ex had over my family even although he did not live with us. He had been in control of me for years when I thought I was getting my life on track.

Another aspect which I still have difficulty getting my head around is the fact that I was sexually abused during my marriage. Having married young, I was quite naive in this department having never been with another man before. During my time with Saje, I remember thinking the week in which we covered the topic of sexual control would not affect me, as this had not happened to me. I sat and listened during the session when all of a sudden it hit me. Yes, I had in fact been affected in this way. I left the group to return home and on the way home I had a massive panic attack. For the next week I could not stop thinking about all the information I had been given and realisation set in that I had in fact been sexually abused. I remember for my birthday one year my ex bought me a lingerie outfit but this was an outfit with zips everywhere. I did not want to put it on yet he insisted. As I stood there I felt like a prostitute, I was so uncomfortable. This was not a birthday present for me, this was one for him.

I often felt like I was his prostitute whenever he wanted sex. I felt used and sometimes felt like he should have left money on the pillow. This was how he made me feel. I felt humiliated and degraded. He would also stand in front of me naked if I was on the phone to family and stand in front of me dangling himself in my face. He thought this was funny.

There were other acts which he did which made me feel cheap, leaving me in tears as I had suffered pain or he had made me feel so used. I am still dealing with these aspects. Trying to get my head around the fact that I was married yet I had also been abused in this way.

I also ended up with genital warts which was a result of him having many affairs which I was not aware of. I remember my GP's words "how many partners have you had in the past?" To which I replied none, he is my first. The GP then said to me, well I would suggest he (my ex) is sleeping with others. As this is how I would have ended up with this condition. I confronted my ex, who assured me this was not the case. However later on I found out this was actually true, so my GP had been right. For the next few years I had to have numerous smear tests to keep a check on my condition. Having digested all this information, I realise if I was put at risk by all his behaviour then so were the many women he had affairs with over the years. This however is not my concern. My concern is dealing with my own issues which were a result of the abuse I suffered. One thing I have learned through this journey is just how strong I am and just how strong my children are.

HERE

IT'S OKAY NOT TO BE OKAY

As I ran across the garden and jumped the fence, the excitement was filling my body, my summer dress and my wellies with my blonde hair scraggly and little twigs sticking in every direction. I could hear my sister giggling behind me as we raced towards the tree house that was so high up in the trees. As we climbed the ladders in through the little door, then slid through the window onto the balcony to watch the cows in the field with the sweets we had just stolen from the kitchen, I couldn't be more happy.

Mum was reading her book in the porch and my dad was in his big tractor busy with the harvest. I eagerly awaited the sound of his tractor horn to give us the signal to run over to the farm with his tea in a box. This was a regular situation. If I was lucky enough I even got to go for a run in the tractor.

My mum and dad were my heroes. As you can gather I was a very happy child. We had a very loving family and my parents were the apple of my eye. I grew up in a beautiful country cottage where we had the run of the estate and by god did I love it. My dad was by far the best role model I could ever have asked for. We did so much together - we laughed, play fought and did so much outdoor stuff, climbing and hill walking.

My childhood in a nutshell was amazing.

So how could things have gone so wrong.

Through my teenage years I became rebellious. I ticked school, I drank at a young age and every weekend me and my bestie hit the town. One thing I did not lose was respect for my parents. I never brought hassle to the door and I was always open with my mum about my relationships with boys. We had such a close bond I could speak to her about anything.

I matured quickly and always had a job from the age of 14. I was a hard grafter. That was the norm for my family. Both my parents grafted and I wanted to do the same. I became qualified in my field of work and got my own place, car and income. Life was great. I was a woman on a mission loving life surrounded by friends and family. What more did I need?

Then he walked into my life…

From day one I could see the signs. I knew he was an ass but his cockiness and charming personality had me drawn in from day one and very quickly I was head over heels. He visited the first night and never left again. That was us, a couple in days. I went to work, he went to work, we spent the evenings together cozied up on the couch watching movies while the cold weather howled outside.

He lost his job. But that was OK, he was looking for another one and the house was clean and tea was made for me coming in although when I was arriving home there were people in my house partying. God I was 19 stop being such an adult, grab a drink and get involved with the party, that's what teenagers do, why was I so stroppy about this stuff. Have fun because in years to come I would regret not pulling sickies because of a terrible hangover.

We got a new house closer to my work and by goodness things were going great. He wasn't hanging about with the same crowd and things were looking really promising. Until I arrived home and my house was ransacked. I'd been robbed… that was my thought. Oh god, we have been robbed. Until I reached my bedroom where there were rose petals in the shape of a heart with an apology... I didn't understand what had happened, what had I done, things were going so well.

I contacted the landlord and said I was so sorry but the place had been trashed. She came down and helped me. I didn't understand why this woman was being so nice. My mum arrived and I packed my belongings and moved back home. We had only been dating 3 months and I'd lost my house.

I was rushing to work. I felt so sick. I missed him. I had no clue what I had done, why he had fallen out with me and he just wouldn't answer. Eventually 4 days later I received a call asking me to go and pick him up. The hurt in his voice broke my heart. I'd never heard him cry. I felt awful. I had been so angry with him and really he had been grieving the anniversary of his family member's passing. I picked him up and to my parents' house he came.

Wait, what happened... as soon as he arrived my mum left. What was she playing at, she always supported me. Why was she walking out on me like this? *I love him,* I told her and she just wouldn't give me an answer.

Things in my life became very complicated in the next few days...I was pregnant. I got engaged but my biggest heart break was my parents told us they were getting divorced. *What the fuck?* I did not see that one coming.

So we upped and moved to his parents' house. His drinking had got worse. I was suffering from black outs, I didn't have my own house, my parents were nowhere to been seen, I was living in a strange woman's house living by her rules, there were people in the house til all times of the night… What had happened to my ideal world? It had literally all gone, but he still loved me and we were going to be a family and things would be OK.

Wham! Holy shit my head was spinning and I could see stars. What the hell just happened? I could not focus properly. He was drunk. "You always said you'd never stay with a man if he hit you so there you go I'VE hit you now pack your bags and get the fuck out."

Hell fucking no I picked up my phone and phoned the police. I've been assaulted and he was bloody well right, no chance at all would I stay with him now, baby daddy or not, no way in hell was I putting up with this… Wrong move. Next thing I knew he was hauling out my clothes… What was he doing? I walked out the room. I needed to check my face which was still stinging, what was that smell, oh Christ he has set my clothes on fire…

This was the first day of the next 6 years.

Marriage, love, children, hurt, pain, rape, poverty, isolation.

I hadn't seen him for a week and as I sat in my house doing my make up listening to Jessie J 'Who you are', the words cut me life a knife.

Brushing my hair, do I look perfect?
I forgot what to do to fit the mold, yeah
The more I try the less it's working, yeah,
Cause everything inside me screams, no, no, no, no,

I put my hands on the dresser and before I knew it my makeup was everywhere. YES where had this girl been for so long the one that had been locked down so far inside, the one with the attitude and the fuck you personality. I walked out my house, pjs still on, straight to

145

the door of the house he was partying in. I walked through the front door took my wedding band off, threw it at him and told him I was done and that he was a fucking monster and he said nothing.

The look in his face was beautiful because I knew in that second he knew I was serious and that made my tummy flutter with a million emotions.

A new house a new start. 6 months had passed. He lived on a drink and drug binge and I though jeezo I should have walked away years ago, this had been so easy, why had I been so scared to leave. I had had no contact with him. He did not want to see the kids. Life was great, my babies were happy and we were moving on, I had even summed up the courage to start dating again.

I had felt very on edge over the last few days but I just couldn't figure out what was wrong. I felt nervous in my own wee house like someone was watching me. I felt like things were moving in my house. I put it down to paranoia and the past 6 years of my life. The kids were at my mum's. I had a night to myself, a little glass of wine while I hopped in the shower with some music on, getting ready for a first date, oh I was excited, the front door was locked and I felt OK. I was a little into my second glass and thought, oh jeezo you're going to have to slow down or you'll be drunk by the time you get there, not a very good first impression ha-ha. Boy did I sober up quickly. Turning off the shower, music still playing, I wrapped my towel round me, walked through the living room and my heart stopped. There he was standing on the balcony. I had no idea how he knew where I lived. All my suspicions were confirmed. It had to have been him. I was quite bad for not locking my patio door, god I was on the second floor - you don't really imagine someone is going to climb up a drain pipe and come into my house. My sofa was two deck chairs. I hardly had anything worthwhile stealing. But there he was staring at me through the glass doors. Through absolute fear, I peed myself. He opened the door and walked in. I was frozen to the spot. There was no way I would be able to lock the door quickly enough. He sat down and picked up my wine glass and sipped away like this was basically his house. I asked him what he wanted, to which he didn't speak. He got up, walked through to my kitchen, picked up my house keys, went to the front door, unlocked it and left. And there in that moment I released how wrong I had been about my simple walk away from the relationship.

My house ended up like a prison. Doors and windows were locked at all times. I got second locks and my house was covered in hidden weapons. There was a golf cub behind the front door and a hammer on the window ledge halfway up the stairs.

The night before my son's birthday there was a loud banging on my front door. It was the back of 11 - who the hell was at my door? I phoned my mum and I did not turn on a single light. I crept through the house to the patio windows. My mum was ready to phone the police if it was him but to my surprise there was a police car sitting in my drive. I raced down the stairs and opened my door to find two officers at my door. They asked if they could come in. I was not at all keen. I trusted no one, let alone the police; they were no help when I had phoned them before. Why did I need them now and what did they want? They came upstairs. I asked them to keep it quiet as my kids were in bed sleeping. They came through the living room and I don't know it was amusement or disbelief, the look on their faces when I offered them a deck chair. *We have reason to believe that you may have been the target of a robbery this evening. Someone phoned in a call to say there was a tall slim built person standing in the bottom garden. They were then watched trying to climb the drain pipe but the person who had been watching asked them if they were OK and they ran off into a vehicle parked at the bottom of the street and took off. Unfortunately, the person who intervened could not make out the type of car or registration plate. Do you know anyone who could be meaning to cause you harm?*

Do I trust these people, do I want them in my house, if I say anything is this going to cause me more hassle?

"No," I replied. "I don't know of anyone."

"Have you lived here long or are you doing repairs?"

Again, I replied "No, my mum helped me decorate when I moved in and this is a council house I don't do the repairs." I soon tried to usher them out the house. I didn't want anyone knowing I had the police in my house.

As they walked down the stairs the officer turned around and looked at me and asked me again, "Are you sure there is no one that you know that could pose a danger to you or your children?"

I was a little concerned that he had seen through my lie. I cleared my throat and said, "No honestly, I can't think of anyone."

He picked up the hammer off the window ledge. "Oh, what handicap are you? "

"What are you talking about," I replied

"The golf club in the corner. I take it you play golf to have a golf club just lying behind your front door."

Well to fuck I have no answer to that one.

Well actually officer my husband is some kind of crazy person who has no problem arriving at my house unannounced and I feel honestly that one day he will kill me. There is a 10 inch blade under my mattress, there are three screwdrivers hidden in my hall, there's a baseball bat inside the huge vase in the living room, there are at least fifteen knifes in the kitchen and I have a crow bar in the bathroom cupboard... Absolutely cannot tell him that!!!!!

"Oh no, my nephew likes to play, he had that one out cleaning it earlier, the rest are in the car."

They left but I had no assurance that they believed a word I had said.

I became a recluse. I didn't want to leave the house, I didn't want to go out with friends, I didn't have friends come to my house in case he turned up and hurt them. I kept my curtains shut. I was living life out of Absolute fear and I wasn't even with him. This made it so much more difficult because I didn't know where he was at any point in time, so going out wasn't an option in case he broke into my house or in case he found me in the street. My epilepsy had hit an all-time high and social work ended up coming in and getting involved to help with the children. Eventually I crumbled. This social worker was so lovely. She was really nice and I felt comfortable speaking to her. I told her all about my husband and the threat he posed against me and the children.

She was an angel in the dark. She got me moved house, I got a home safety check, they gave me bars for my doors and safety lights for the front and back of my house. I was closer to my mum. They fitted alarms inside my house for my epilepsy but they also got the domestic abuse unit to put alarms on both my address house number and mobile number.

It didn't take long before he found me again and the cycle kept repeating itself.

This is when I was introduced to Saje. Things started to dramatically change in my life. I realised I was not to blame and that he was probably never going to change. I found an inner strength. Speaking to women who had also been though what I had been through. I felt like I had found my calling. By week three I was looking at my facilitator thinking that is what I want to be doing with my life.

I completed my groups and started volunteering. I had passion and enthusiasm again. I wanted to help people the way the Saje had helped me. Within a few months I had a paid employment and I have never looked back.

We have had no contact with him at all in the past 3 years and I also found the courage to challenge him through court when he decided he wanted access. Once he realised I was not backing down he gave up and did not pursue me through court.

Then he walked into my life…

This incredible man. A role model just like my dad was to me as a child. Caring and supportive and by my side through all the good times and the bad times. My kids adore him. Now known as Dad in our household, we got a house together, our dogs and our kids. 5 years on and the only thing he does that annoys me is eat crisps in bed but I'll take that any day. ☺

THE LOVE I DESERVED

Darkness was my only light
My days were filled with grey
I had no fight left in me
My days just faded away

So long I had forgotten
How life was meant to be
To have someone to hold me
Feel safe warm and free

The kids were my only handle
They were all I had to grip
That's when you found us
And I felt that handle slip

If there was ever a sign
That was surely one
The battles I had been fighting
Could be challenged and won

Thank goodness for the car show
Who really would have thought
I'd meet the love of my life
Parked in the end spot

All joking aside
There is so much more to say
The role you've taken on
The kids loved you more each day

The memories we have made
And the laughs we all have had
Are only because of one thing
You're an amazing outstanding loving dad

POWER

I met Shithead when I was 17 and living in a children's hostel after leaving home. He was tall and had tattoos, he was the typical 'bad boy' teenage girls swoon over. The first night we spent together was amazing! We sat up and talked all night, I had never laughed so much. I thought I had found my soulmate. At this point he was already in a relationship with someone else but told me he would finish it with her because he felt the same about me. He treated me well at the beginning and took me to meet all his family, which at 17 was such a big step I thought he must really love me. I moved in with him and his mum just before my 18th birthday and when we got our own place together, I thought I had it made. Shithead quickly became controlling and aggressive which I mistook for protective and passionate. He stopped me from seeing my friends and even limited the time I could spend with my mum, who had suffered a stroke the year before. A few months later we had moved back in with his mum and I discovered that he was cheating on me. At this point I'd had enough and told him I was leaving him. I went out with my friends drinking that night and Shithead contacted me during the night and asked if we could meet to talk. When I met up with him, he was drunk. He grabbed me and shoved me in the car and drove us back to his mum's. It was then that we started arguing again. I was frustrated that he wasn't even sorry for cheating on me, so I pushed him when he turned his back on me. That was it, he flew into a rage and started punching me in the face and grabbing my hair. As I ran away, he caught up with me and slammed my head into the pavement and broke my nose. I was bleeding and scared so I ran back to his mum's flat but she had locked the door. He ran up the stairs and started kicking and choking me and that's when a neighbour saw what was happening and called the police. After that incident I was so

153

confused. How could a man that claims to love me do this to me? I wanted to see him to get answers and the first thing he said to me when I called was, "How bad is your face? Put make up on to cover it up. I don't want to see it." He apologised and cried, blaming me for pushing him first and told me his abusive childhood was what made him violent and lash out sometimes. He promised it would never happen again and I believed him.

A few months down the line, I got a job in a bar. I had only been there a matter of days before Shithead started calling me and turning up out of the blue. I was given a warning by my boss and told I couldn't have visitors at work. When I told Shithead this, he lost it. He started sitting outside my work and watching me through the window. He would accuse me of sleeping with customers he saw me talking to. In September 2008 I found out I was pregnant and told him he would have to change or I would be leaving him. I went to work as normal and had a phone call from him an hour or so later. He told me he had taken an overdose because he couldn't live without me. I left work that night and never returned. Throughout the pregnancy he was paranoid and jealous and never bothered coming to scans or midwife appointments. He would go drinking with friends and stay out for days at a time. I had gone from a bubbly, happy teenager to a submissive, nervous wreck. The few friends I still had left noticed this change in me and begged me to leave him. His family assured me that once the baby was here he would settle down and change his ways. This was not the case.

We moved into our own place just before my eldest was born. He decorated the whole place and for a while he was the doting father and partner. I fell pregnant with my middle child only 6 weeks afterwards and we were excited to learn it was another girl. Halfway through my pregnancy I found out he was cheating on me again. I kicked him out and he got his own place. He seemed to sort himself out and again I took him back. We remained in separate houses but were always together. We started doing things as a family and going out on dates. Slowly the abuse crept up on me again. He would fly off the handle for the smallest of reasons. If he didn't like what I'd made for dinner he would throw it across the room and make me clean it up. If I took too long at the shops he would pin me against the wall and demand to know where I 'really' was and who I'd been with. If he was going out, he would have his mum come round to keep an eye on me "for my sake". I wasn't allowed to go anywhere without an escort. The cheating continued and he stopped trying to hide it. He would sit on the phone, in front of me, and talk about the girls he had been meeting and what they were like in bed. It was then that I found out I was expecting my youngest child. I was at breaking point and didn't know if I could go through it all again. I considered terminating the pregnancy, but Shithead talked me out of it. He said he would stop cheating and go to anger management. He blamed depression for the way he had been acting and even went to the doctor to get medication. During the pregnancy we were living separately but made a go of our relationship. Just a year after my son was born Shithead had convinced me to move in with him and give up my flat. After an argument one morning, he kicked me out of the flat with no money or phone. I walked into town and made my way to the women's refuge. I told them what had been going on over the last five years and they offered me and the children a room. With a police escort, I headed back to the flat and collected the kids and some of our things. That was the start of my journey to leaving.

After leaving I used alcohol to cope and to block out the feelings of guilt and shame. I blamed myself for going back time and time again. When I stopped drinking, I stopped eating and lived off coffee and cigarettes for months. I finally got back in contact with a couple of friends and told them what had been going on. I applied for a house of my own with the children and eventually moved out of the refuge.

Shithead still saw the kids, when he could be bothered, but would turn up at my house out of the blue demanding I let him in to see who was there. Leave the kids with his mum and sit outside my flat or follow me around wherever I went. It was at that point I stopped him from having the children overnight and contact became sporadic. He would only want to see the children if I was there and told me it was important we all spend time together as a family. This went on for months. He stalked and harassed me, which resulted in the police being called numerous times. In June after a night out he broke into my flat and threatened to kill me. The next day I moved myself and my kids back into the refuge and booked a one-way ticket to the UK. We left in 2013 and have never looked back. I gave Shithead the chance to see the kids with a legal contact agreement I had drawn up through a solicitor. Within months he had broken the agreement and has not seen or spoken to the kids in five years. A few months after moving, I started with Saje's group and it changed my life. It showed me that I wasn't responsible for the abuse and helped me better understand what I had been through. It was reassuring to know I wasn't alone and after completing group, I decided to start volunteering for Saje to help other victims of domestic abuse. The two years that I worked with Saje were fantastic. Not only was I helping other women; I was also helping myself. Five years after leaving my abuser, I am now settled in a beautiful house, I have a full-time job and my children are happy, healthy and safe.

LOVE

#FREEDOM

Surely My Prince Charming,
(With his smile oh-so disarming)
Would not be happy harming
All that makes me ME!
His drip of poison was insidious,
The reality truly hideous.
As my friends they saw his viciousness,
I'd to drop them one by one.

Meant to be my Man,
But you'd do anything you can,
To undermine my sanity,
And bash and bruise my vanity.
'Coz my banter was flirting,
Going out was called" shirking",
In shadows you'd be lurking,
Waiting to teach me
Your lesson.

You'd shame me,
Then blame me.
Clout me, doubt me
Then try and mount me.
1year…still not clear,
If I should even be here.
2year…so many hot tears,
And brand new fears,
With your name on.

Your mates were thugs,
Ugly mugs, Staffie dugs
And painful heart-string tugs.
No low cut, no make-up,
You yell: I crumble.
This is one warped kinda humble,
Dunno what way's up
As I trip and stumble.

A prediction of addiction,
A definite predilection
For Class A drugs.
It was really no wonder,
(And I sometimes ponder)
That it didn't happen sooner.
And now you've got,
The perfect rod,
To beat my back with…
Hard!

#FREEDOM
Come to us and get some, of the space you might need
To cry, to bleed: To succeed!
A safe, secure place,
Where it isn't a race
And everyone roots for you.
A work in progress, not to regress
No perfection: Progress.

THE SPACES IN BETWEEN

NOTE: This chapter shows only excerpts of my story. Like all the stories in this book, it is full of spaces: gaps in memory; events too painful to remember; things I'd rather forget. In my case, each ellipsis can be substituted for a dozen tiny and huge moments across a long period of time. Complicated family scenarios involving estrangement and strained relationships with my own family, including my children, each time instigated by my husband's unreasonable behaviour. Recurrent arguments where my own behaviour and very nature was constantly scrutinized while he retained immunity. Difficult and humiliating scenes enacted in public and in private. Countless trips and supposed holidays where seemingly insignificant details triggered his full-blown and long-lasting feuds with others. My subsequent anguish in trying to deal with the fallout of all of the above. If any of our stories seem incomplete, it's because of this: every moment leads on from the last, every past argument informing the next. It is impossible to tell the full story. The spaces in between - the words not spoken - are just as important. Eventually, to try to even begin to understand and move through and past an abusive relationship, we must deconstruct every single moment that got us there. This book gives just a glimpse of what that process means…

…

My daughter Lucy had a big hand in my meeting up with a new man in my life in my fifties. We were both in care services and he held a very senior position. I'd been on my own for 11 years having been divorced from a very difficult marriage. I wasn't actively looking for a partner but did feel ready to be in a relationship again.

160

A message from him (I'll call him "James" here) on my answerphone set my heart racing. He invited me to dinner when I called him back and the scene was set. The evening was successful despite my nerves and we got on well, and on the next date we found we had many shared interests, sport, music, career, and religion. James was charming, intelligent, witty in fact quite bewitching. A CD of Billy Fury 'Halfway to Paradise' followed in the post. I was hooked.

When we first met, I was working full time in a managerial role in the care sector. I was hard working, very committed to my job and had a good circle of friends. I liked travelling abroad, eating out, reading, walking and time with family. I had my own home and car and was grateful for my health and a decent standard of living.

There were so many romantic gestures in those early days: love notes in books, numerous texts daily with love song quotes, talking for hours on the phone and tracing a huge heart in the sand on the beach. It was a wild kind of intimacy between us.

He met my family and my son, Alex, told him, "you'd better take care of my mother." They all thought he was great. I felt so lucky. He said it was providential.

The relationship moved on very quickly. I was spending weekends at his home. On holiday in the Canaries he proposed, and my dreams fulfilled when we got engaged in Paris with him on bended knee.

There were some subtle incidents in the first six months - travelling to visit his brother, James braked hard to avoid another car at a roundabout, leaving me gasping for breath. He snapped and swore at me and immediately I was in tears. He did apologise, one of the few times that he did and I dismissed it.

Before our first holiday he made a strange remark that he thought I would be a three star person whilst he was four. Again, I let it go.

One Friday evening he was preparing fish and I told him I'd arranged a meal for us and my brother and his wife. He spun round, glaring at me and in a very cold tone told me not to make any plans for him without checking. I was very shaken and said I thought he would be pleased to meet up. The message was clear, I'd crossed a line. However, I let it pass thinking he's right I shouldn't have done that.

Our first Christmas was lovely though he found all the gifts exchanged was excessive. In January my daughter and partner were starting on a two year visit to Australia. The night they left I stayed at James's house and I was up during the night sad and weepy. James came rushing through the hall saying I'd frightened him; he wondered where I was. I explained it was due to my sadness of my daughter going off for such a long time. He said his late wife used to turn on the tears, and it was emotional incontinence. We wrangled about it for hours! I nearly walked out, I was so anxious. Another message that he didn't deal very well with tears. It was a week before he got in touch. I was so relieved. I thought I'd blown it.

I didn't recognise the impact of the negative remarks James made about TV programmes I liked, yet I stopped watching them and my favourite 'Sounds of the Sixties' radio programme he said was just the B sides of records! I believed him, he was more informed and intelligent than me. Eventually I stopped putting it on. Comments about giving up work, that he'd look after me if my savings ran out, seemed so caring.

I did notice James liked to talk and was a good conversationalist, and would regale me with stories during his career which I could identify with. He talked a lot about his late wife which I put down to

162

unresolved grief. It was clear James liked an audience to listen to his opinions on any subject particularly politics and football. He had a big personality. And I noted he listened poorly when I spoke and could effortlessly shift the conversation back to himself. Being a reserved person, I was content to listen, I'm good at that. So, in a way I was the perfect foil for him.

...

James had been on a trip abroad with a friend and I was picking him up, I was unsure of airport parking and sent a text advising James I'd be outside. As soon as he was in the car, he launched into a scathing reprimand that he'd been looking forward all weekend to me greeting him in arrivals. His angry outburst was so unexpected I was in tears trying to explain and apologise for my mistake. He later put his temper down to painful constipation. I blamed myself for not being more organised.

It was on our first holiday that James's walking problem manifested and on our return he reluctantly agreed to see his GP and was diagnosed with a spinal condition and sent for physio. He researched the Internet and was convinced he had MS or MND. By this time, I was spending most of my time at his house taking on more of the household tasks and I'd mooted we sell up and buy a house together. He wouldn't agree to that, insisting his property was private, large, in the leafy suburbs and well maintained, no need to move. I could rent out my flat.

I'd shared some of my deepest vulnerabilities with James including fears about money. In the future, he would throw these back in my face. I'd suggested a joint account which he dismissed, as he didn't trust me yet.

Things began to change.

I moved in with James 18 months after we'd met. I rented out my flat. I'd discussed taking some things with me to help me adjustment and James came and selected items which he thought would fit in and exchanged some new pieces of mine with old ones of his. We discussed finance and instead of pooling monies he suggested I contribute to the household expenses, he'd worked out a figure. I felt awkward about it, however it became routine that I'd give him a cheque at the end of the month. We had been splitting entertainment costs e.g. cinema/ theatre tickets, hotel bills, coffees etc. This routine continued with me paying half all household purchases curtains, carpets, upgrade of bathrooms and most furniture had been replaced. We paid for our own clothes, hairdressing, toiletries and all holidays together. I felt like a tenant.

...

That night James cuddled up to me in bed, relief flooding through me. I blamed it all on his disability; he was recovering from spinal surgery. Later, he confided that he had bullied his wife into submission. Secretly I thought, *that's what happens to me*. I chose a calm moment and asked how I should respond when he got angry, what would be more helpful to him? He advised that I tell him how I was feeling even though he might not like what I had to say.

...

Bewildering hostile episodes occurred regularly followed by a calm period. The venting was familiar. Swearing and demeaning remarks: "No wonder your ex drank, you have an abusive personality, you have a lacuna in your brain' (I had to look that up - it means a gap.) My explanations were dismissed by threats that if I didn't change we were finished. I was on edge all the time. He often talked about his parents never attending his prize-givings, no support from them and saying that's how I made him feel when I went off on an impulse. I'd feel guilty and think I had been nippy. He was right. I'd have to try harder.

Christmas Eve I'd queued to buy some handmade chocs, James was waiting in the car. I came outside and he grabbed my arm, angrily stating he'd been waiting frozen for half an hour. I was insensitive, had a block in my brain. I apologised and felt sick. Punishing silence followed, we went to midnight mass and retired to bed with James turned away on the other side of the bed. I felt very low and anxious. Christmas day he came round slowly.

We went to Australia in January for my daughter's wedding, renting a flat. I was badly bitten by mosquitos as I sat on the balcony during the night with jet lag. James was furious, where was my head? I needed to visit A & E for dressings and was given antibiotics. My daughter had organised an itinerary of events for guests who travelled from Britain. James was subdued and bad tempered. He wouldn't attend outdoor bowls, BBQ's, beach party, meals at friends' homes. James sullenly said nothing was suitable for him with his disability, making hurtful remarks about the organisation yet everyone else had really enjoyed the activities. Somehow, when life wasn't revolving around James, he'd be resentful. James disappeared all day before the wedding avoiding the drinks party. I found him drinking in the flat. Accusations were hurled. He wished he hadn't come!

The wedding was outdoors in a beautiful setting, I gave a short speech. Wow, James congratulated me on it. We had to leave early as James was fixated on getting a taxi home.

My daughter had organised a surprise trip for us on a small plane to north beach for a meal. A thank you for our support. James refused to go. He didn't like surprises, what a waste of money, he said. I was gutted, such a kind thought being trashed. I tried to cover it up, kept cool and blamed James's disability.

Back home James referred to the debacle that occurred, him limping around, he couldn't cope with it and resolved that I'd go on my own next time. He said he gets angry at them, becomes aggressive and insulting and silences me, even admitting he could be hard and cruel. A rare moment of owning his behaviour and my hopes were high.

...

I had cut my work days to 4 then 3 after my back injury and pressure from James. A complicated issue arose at work with a very disturbed family. James was an experienced and skilled negotiator, and he was instrumental in the lengthy process of vindicating my actions. I decided to retire at the end of the year. His help has been at the top of James's list of favours. He raises the incident over and over again to prove his superiority and contribution to our relationship.

...

In July my young niece's husband took his own life in tragic circumstances. James and I visited next day with food I'd cooked. James was angry as I'd wanted to return again, how did I know I was welcome, whose needs was I meeting. I didn't go but phoned every day.

Driving to the crematorium, James was berating me as I was unsure of directions. People had gathered at my brother's house afterwards. Driving home, James criticised the service. At home he was tearful and angry talking about his father. Later he questioned my behaviour re: going to see the family, wanting to return to see them, then changing my mind. When I tried to explain he'd been angry, James shouted that now it's all his fault I didn't go, me blaming him, acting out. I reminded him of his temper and swearing. He was stabbing his finger at me shouting he'd been ignored by my brother in his home, no social skills and left alone for 38 mins, accusations of disloyalty, lack of trust, never had this problem before. I'd no insight into my bad bitch behaviour, I was f****d up, didn't want me in his bed I could go to the spare room. Amid distress, my head a mass of confusion, I asked did he want to split up. He replied, not yet but maybe in the future.

...

Our 5th Christmas, a disaster, started off well, my brother and family, my son all gathered happily, James the congenial host, witty and charming. I invited my son Alex's friend to join us for dinner without checking with James. In the kitchen, he coldly confronted me with - how dare I invite someone to dinner without checking with him. My apology met with, "F****** cow!!!" Despite my pleas, James spent the evening locked in the en-suite for several hours in a burning rage whilst I apologised to our guests for causing a domestic. The impact and consequences of "my mistake" were to last for years. I was banished to the spare room following an onslaught of demeaning insults and threats. I was sick with fear, next day my son was ordered to meet him at a hotel in town where James blamed him for what had happened. He was abusive and threatening towards Alex, demanding he collect any belongings from the house. James's appalling behaviour lasted for weeks, he said he'd had to remain in the en-suite as he'd lost control wanting to beat up my son saying he was a psychopath and needed stopping. I was broken, I even tried to persuade my son to say sorry to make it all go away, although distressed Alex didn't agree to my pleading. He was right, of course. He'd done nothing wrong. James would use this episode to taunt me many times.

...

The rejection I felt with silence was torture. Once James didn't talk to me for five weeks. I'd picked my lip causing it to bleed and James came for breakfast and raged at me saying he had to look at my face. I'd stay in, wanting to please, clean everything in sight, working in the garden. I learned he would only talk when he was ready, which entailed a post mortem of the event, cleverly shifting blame: it was a pattern of mine, it had to stop, we'd give it three months and see how we were. I struggled to figure out what was happening. I talked it out with a friend and decided it wasn't normal and maybe there was a mental health problem.

...

The impact of my increasingly isolated life was noted by family and friends, as I made excuses to avoid invitations to meet up for fear of recriminations. My loss of weight was evident, and my son remarked how distracted I appeared and how I didn't laugh much anymore.

Finance had always been fraught with anxiety. At James's request I gave him a monthly cheque for my contribution to household expenses and a list of other household monies spent by either of us which James checked and then adjusted accordingly the final amount. Most furniture in the house was halved. I felt like a tenant. It was James's house when he was angry and ours when he was calm.

...

The beginning of my awareness of the problem.

James often said I had a dysfunctional relationship with my son and needed counselling. In the end I said OK I'll go. He backtracked, protesting I didn't need it.

At the first session the terms, control and coercion were raised. I didn't understand the relevance to me. I said to the counsellor she was only hearing my side, she replied firmly, 'I've heard enough'. She suggested I go online and read about it.

During the night I used James's I-Mac and was shocked when I scrolled down the warning signs of coercion. I shut it down afraid James would know I'd been on the site.

One day my son asked me if he could store some boxes at the house and I agreed. James was furious how dare I, I'd no right to agree, my son should come through him, the boxes never came! In bed James cuddled up to me declaring his love wanting us to communicate better no anger, he needed to support my son. What a turnaround... it didn't last.

The counsellor pointed out James needed to come for help but sent me instead. She said I'd only a sliver of space in the marriage whilst James had a huge chunk. She had spoken to Women's Aid. I'd never heard of them, they were the experts she said and I should contact them.

From then on I started researching and learning a lot about control and narcissism, in particular a sense of entitlement.

Christmas dinner almost finished, my brother called and I spoke for ten minutes. James was scathing in his response. He'd had to clear up

I'd talked so long, shouting I shouldn't have taken the call. He drank a couple of whiskies, went to bed smashing a wedding picture over the floor.

With James asleep I picked up all the glass in case he'd cut his feet. Next morning he came to breakfast and stood beating his chest, saying 'I feel great today'. I was astonished. It was as though nothing had ever happened.

...

Lucy my daughter and family came from Oz to stay with us. Problems arose before they arrived, resulting in James often silent and hostile to me. I left for a few days and decided to attend Women's Aid. It was a huge step for me. The woman on duty, Davina, was young - how could she help me! She said I'd been dismantled, I was shocked to learn women can leave and return 7 or 8 times. She explained the cycle of abuse - 6 days out of 7 the man could be abusive and on the 7th day charming and loving. The woman relieved, she tells herself, *see he does love me after all*. I could identify with that. As a result of painful incidents during Lucy's holiday, she and my son became estranged from James.

I recall an incident when James used old information I'd disclosed, in a cruel emotional attack about baggage I'd brought re my father and ex-husband. I'd been sobbing on our bed and he came and sat stroking my back. I was grateful and confused by the comfort and attention from James when he was actually the perpetrator of this mental torture. I learned in time from Davina that this was just a different approach to his control, as these times of kindness gave me hope that he would change.

...

170

Christmas came. I went early to see my grandchildren. I returned to find a note from James, a poem about a broken heart and bible quote about casting the first stone. On return we ate Christmas dinner in silence, yet he said I was a good cook.

I gave him gifts, he refused them. I cleared up and watched TV, James in the study. At bedtime James appeared angry and demanding I return his note. When I wouldn't, he became very aggressive, he grabbed me and pinned me in the corner, he was shouting in my face where was the note and threatening me, I was very frightened I'd be hurt, he came at me again gripping my arms against the wall. He told me to get out, swearing and insulting name calling. I went to get things for the spare room, he was still ranting as he followed me around, eventually going to bed. I went to the spare room, wedged a chair against the door fearful he might return. When I thought James was asleep, I packed some things in my car resolving to leave in the morning. At 1:30 am I heard James shouting for help, found him lying face down across the bed, said he'd blacked out, he was afraid, did I think he was psychotic talking at length about his despair. We were both crying, he had an episode of cardiac arrhythmia which had happened before after work in the garden. He pleaded that I come into bed beside him. Exhausted I did give in and he cuddled up. I lay awake most of night.

At breakfast he came with a lovely Christmas card and put on one of my favourite CDs. I told him how frightened I was by his actions the night before. He said calmly that I had caused it, that I could have been killed last night. I berated myself for not giving him the note. I didn't leave.

...

I doubted my reality. These changes in mood were so confusing yet gave me hope and kept the dream alive.

…

I met regularly with Davina at Women's Aid. She explained about the cycle of abuse and James venting his anger was part of it, as was the charming seductive witty man I glimpsed at times. She was very concerned about my safety following James's Christmas incident and remarks next morning. James's behaviour was escalating and Davina said it could be a dangerous time for me, and to have an emergency bag available. I started to look at storage costs and renting a flat.

Following a stressful trip, I secretly negotiated my return to the flat, the lease was up and painting organised. Next day I was in the bath using the land line, talking of moving out and storage. James came to get the phone, then called me to the lounge recalling a dream where his late wife told him to look after me. He was willing to see a counsellor, a breakthrough I thought. More brow beating and accusations, me defending. I was afraid to tell him I was leaving, secretly packing. I talked of a new beginning, and reminded him he'd told me to leave many times. He said it was in the heat of the moment.

My friend said James was messing with my head, I was wavering. I had to remember the bad times, nothing would change. My head said leave, my heart still loved him.

James had overheard my phone call talking about him, threatening he'd take me to court for defamation, his anger was the result of serious provocation.

On Sunday my spiritual reading was illuminating - God's voice guides me to talk with others I trust and go forward with life. At the 'Sign of Peace ' (a handshake or embrace) James turned away from me. He'd never done that before. I felt such rejection. Amid my tears I said to myself I'm going to leave today. It was very clear.

After lunch, I told James I wanted to talk to him about our difficulties and strain of recent months, continually being told to leave, this seemed once too many. Despite his protests I spent several hours packing my car, James sat in the lounge, he wanted to talk over dinner, I declined and went forward touching his shoulder to say goodbye.

...

I told my son I'd left a few days later, I hadn't wanted to involve family and hadn't told them anything. He was very surprised yet felt uplifted, said I'd become so diminished my life had shrunk, no joy in it, and now I was so skinny and looked awful. He said James had been bullying and controlling me for years, and caused such trauma in our family relationships. James had said time I spent with family was excessive, in fact it was minimal. Next day I called my daughter in Oz. She had been very angry at James over the last six months, said James knows how to press my buttons, his thinking is so skewed. She was very relieved I'd left, was proud of me.

James called several times. I didn't answer. He sent long cryptic e-mails. I replied explaining why I'd left, how I felt, no longer willing to accept his behaviour. Offered to meet for coffee to look at a way forward.

I arranged and paid for afternoon tea in a lovely venue. James wanted me to return that day, I declined, I needed time. He was very concerned about my health and emotional stability. He raised old issues and I suggested marriage guidance, James had reservations. He was furious about my invitations to join family on holiday, all downhill after that. I asked him to lower his voice - people were looking at us. I said I was going to leave. He called me after 20 minutes, said he'd been angry and left in bad terms. We met in a Gastropub and after threats to get the lawyers involved if I was stringing him along, he agreed to check out psychotherapists on the Internet.

James booked with the church organisation I'd used before (I wanted him to take the initiative to show his commitment). The therapist asked if there was any abuse, I said no. James said no physical but plenty of verbals from him. She thanked him for saying that. She said James spoke to me in a very superior way and put me down several times. I was quiet and hidden. Sadly after two good sessions her husband died suddenly and we were allocated Martha.

Whilst waiting for counselling to start again, we met at a jazz concert at the festival. James was tugging at my heartstrings, asking for hugs and holding me tight with an intimate kiss. I was very uncomfortable, unable to say no. I felt lonely and miserable, for two pins I could have gone home with him. I missed the familiar house, the company, yet it had been unbearable at times.

First session of counselling, James painted me as the wonderful wife, very caring and I expressed the joy and excitement of our relationship, the dream that's now shattered. She talked of the loop we were caught in. James feels rejected by my family, shut out, side-lined and angry which triggers me to be afraid and withdraw, and me now setting a boundary not acceptable to shout and swear. The worm has turned - her words. James said he thought I had an organic brain disorder because my behaviour was so strange, what a put down.

During the next session I revealed I couldn't look to James for emotional support and that he would be angry when I was crying, giving her some examples of that. He agreed. I'd opened up about control and abuse, James said the idea of it had negative connotations for him yet admitted he felt remorse. She thanked him for being brave.

...

He asked me to come and stay overnight before a trip to visit his old uncle who I liked very much. I brought food and cooked for us there. Despite all my efforts to comfort him James dwelled on his grievances and low mood and kept me talking for hours on end talking in riddles that he felt like Barabas in the bible. I felt sorry for him. When I wanted to return to my flat, he became angry, accusing me of running away again. I tried the deescalating strategies Martha had suggested to no avail. He said it made him feel rejected and controlled, yet I was being manipulated and intimidated. I told him I wouldn't be coming back unless he stopped these angry, aggressive outbursts, insults and put downs.

...

In our first session after Christmas I talked of past events and James slid off it stating he'd never had an experience like this before, no one had ever described him in these terms, and I'd done terrible things to him, worse than anyone in his life. Later in February we went on holiday to Spain together. Once there, I spent some time checking out bus travel to various places, but James was reluctant to join me on any sightseeing trips. I ended up going on my own, dealing with silences, horrible mimicking accusations and insulting demeaning remarks over the course of the week. On our return I'd

175

stayed the night at James's house with him cuddled up feeling cold after the sun.

...

James talked of not coming first with me and at times felt demeaned. I said he was always first in my life, but sometimes someone else was the priority, that being his wife didn't mean I had to forsake all others, I wasn't willing to do that. He had said in the past he needed to be first, second and third in my hierarchy, and wasn't willing to share me.

...

When out for coffee it was always my turn to pay despite me bringing food to cook all weekend when I stayed at his house. He jibed that I wanted to live with him for nothing as I was a mean selfish bitch, and when I walked away and packed to go home I said I felt hurt and disappointed that he'd insulted me. I didn't want to live there for nothing but I wanted to be treated as his wife and I said married women shouldn't have to pay rent. He came back with cutting remarks about no role models in my family to go by with finance. I told him to stop insulting my family and he said you also are mean and selfish as I left.

...

We were discussing plans for a trip to London. James remarked on his superior psychiatric knowledge. He'd organised the therapy and he'd had to guide the therapist in the way forward. He rubbished me, blaming 'flooding'. [Our therapist Martha had described the brain's response when I was faced with James's anger, unable to think and stressed. I become paralysed, blood floods the brain and I can't marshal my thoughts. James wasn't in tune with that. Many times in the future when he was in a rage, James would sneer and shout at me saying 'oh you'll be flooding now', rubbishing this phenomenon]. James said it was me being silent, which I denied. He claimed abuse was something most people do when angry in an argument and conflict. He reminded me of all his efforts to mark anniversaries, birthdays, special days, trips, but what had I done? He has this remarkable ability to exaggerate his good deeds whilst minimising my input.

...

The next couple of weekends at James's were pleasant overall. He raised the date of my return. I knew I wasn't ready to throw in the towel and was stalling, causing James to be cold and angry. I finally picked a date for the next week. He hoped my family would be constructive and not interfere or expect me to do things with them at the drop of a hat. I said they'd never interfered, and I'd be going to spend Tuesday evenings and sleep over at my son's each week. He said some reconciliation with them would be helpful, yet he made no attempt to contact my son or daughter saying I should help with that.

I talked to Davina about my decision, revealing I felt ashamed and weak going back, and letting her down after all the time she had spent with me. She said it's what I needed to do, the cycle is continuing and I'm still minimising it, but I'm more vocal and a threat to James each time I stood up to him. She was worried about me falling back into old habits, checking my watch when I'm with friends or the children. It can happen very quickly, James is very possessive of me, in the guise that I'm safe and secure with him.

I returned to live with James in June, with my flat rented out. We went on holiday to his cousin's in the Islands where I was always made so welcome. Sunday morning in the cottage ruined by James angry and nasty, blaming me for not waking him for church as he was dozing in the chair. I felt nervous and shaken when we picked up his cousin. James was charming with her. Later we were in her house across the track and James had gone to the cottage finding I'd locked the door by mistake. He returned very angry and swearing at me in the hall. I was shocked. He was silent watching football. I tried to lighten the atmosphere, chatting to his cousin. In bed later James was all for cuddling up as though nothing had occurred.

…

He was angry about a ladder in the garage I'd borrowed from a friend who was on holiday so I couldn't return it. He said unkindly I hadn't asked permission to leave it in the garage and I said but I live here. James replied coldly it wasn't my house, I had my flat, and he wouldn't wait again for me disappearing down the drive with my helper's advice. He added threateningly… if I used the "abuse" word again I'd be gone, adding nastily that I was a very quirky woman with odd behaviours. These sessions were frequent and exhausting. He used his power in sinister little subtle ways to undermine my stability. Some days it seemed I was living in a war zone on high alert, waiting for the next grenade. He said his intentions were always for the best, yet ending up spewing out old stuff, beating me down for my lack of affection. The last two weeks had been like a roller coaster. I did minimise the impact of these punishing attacks, then apologise for getting angry. In bed, again I allowed him to massage my back despite it feeling very strange and my head a bit crazy.

…

He left me a note, 'Thought for the day', about how past hurts take time to heal and for trust to be re-established. We needed tolerance and sensitivity. A good marriage required a united effort to succeed and a belief in the sacrament. My thought for the day was that would be great if it was followed up with action.

...

At dinner he was annoyed at a news report about violence at home, saying, "where's the evidence - there's no evidence when it's emotional or psychological abuse." Later he was being all sweet, preparing the nights' viewing, his chair near mine. James was all ready for bed and showered. I was reading and he started to play Elvis songs - seduction honeymoon stuff.

...

Middle of November I raised The Serious Conversation. James was vague, saying what conversation? James reluctantly started off when I'd returned in June - and went to give a potted history of all the past issues, me going out doing my own thing, no discussion or thought for him. I said we'd dealt with all these issues in the counselling, James dismissed that as nonsense.

Next day I was getting ready to go to work in the charity shop. James made a sarcastic remark about it, I think annoyed I'd be going to Al Anon later. He said I rushed back from the shop and out to the meeting bleating to women there, then I fell asleep and up during the night, what about the impact on him. "You're My Wife, you act as though you're entitled to do what you want." I said I'm not out drinking or seeing someone else. He said he didn't care, I'd a history of running away. I said he'd told me to leave, and he said F*** off then. He became very angry, saying I'd accused him of things in writing. I said I told you how I felt. He said he didn't care how I felt, he'd "Like to Take a Knife to my Throat and Cut it… and You Can Tell That to your friends." He was standing above me pointing his finger at me, accusing me of breaking my marriage vows three times and blaming me for his angry and contemptuous mood. I stood up angrily and picked up my plate. James jumped back from me. I put the plates in the dishwasher saying to stop it James, stop it. He went off to the lounge.

James had nothing to eat that night complaining he wasn't feeling well. Next morning he said he wanted me to sleep in the spare room saying we were disturbing each other. I said I'd think about it, he said starting tonight. I felt sick, stomach churning, mouth dry. I met a friend for a chat, who was very supportive. James's uncle arrived unexpected and James was very chatty to him as though all was hunky dory, returning to silent mode after he'd gone.

Davina was very concerned about James's threat re: the knife and that he'd delivered it in a rational calm way. She said abuse always escalates as the person gains strength, being more derogatory, it's intended to crush me till I don't have any fight left. I said I hadn't felt afraid. Maybe I was defiant yet I do normalise things and she described how I'd told her in a matter of fact manner with no affect at all and she was taken aback by that.

…

James had written down some notes he wanted to discuss. I reminded him of a variety of things of things I'd organised, how unless James is interested, he won't go. Whereas if he suggests something, I'll go even if I don't care for it. I mentioned the last aggressive outburst and was crying. James sneered how could he talk to me when I'm like that, meaning my tears. I emphasised how afraid I was. He didn't deny any of it. I said I couldn't take much more, it was breaking me and had to stop. He opined, what if he was mentally ill, he couldn't be blamed, if someone was killed and was found to be not guilty on grounds of insanity.

Davina gave me copies of material from a book by Lundy Bancroft about perpetrators of abuse at my next session. I ordered it that week. The book described control and abuse so clearly, it became a very important support for me.

…

On our way to church James asked about the booking [there'd been a mix-up on my holiday booking]. I said I'd fixed it and had to get my ticket re-issued. He was angry I hadn't told him earlier after me getting him to go on the Internet at midnight, mimicking me for whining and being sorry for myself. He started to rant on. He worried about me, I was a vindictive bitch. I told him to stop it, he kept on raging, me not intelligent enough to book my flight. I said not to speak to me like that and his shouting got worse swearing at me to F*** off. I said to stop the car and let me out. He said don't dare do anything stupid, just sit there and have a think what you're doing, in two hours he'd have my belongings out of the house. He drove very fast towards a T - junction, I was very scared shouting to stop, there were cars coming, he slammed on the brakes skidding up to the junction. I didn't say any more. I felt hopeless and despairing.

The more I have challenged him the more his behaviour has deteriorated. It's been a continuous barrage of insults baiting me. I reach a point where I react with anger.

That night James asked if I would come back to his bed. I agreed I would as long as he didn't mind if I had a disturbed night. James cuddled up close.

I had breakfast and was finishing packing for my trip when James got up. He came into the spare room asking for my house keys. He'd asked for them several days before and I didn't return them. I replied I needed them to get back into the house. He went for my handbag, emptied it onto the bed and took my keys. He called me a thief. I kept quiet and went for a shower.

James was in the lounge, I took my cases to the utility room and went to ask for a key, he refused saying he'd be here. I said I was afraid he'd change the locks or sell up. He said he wouldn't break his word.

The taxi came I'd to ask James to open the door, I put my hand into his gilet pocket and found my keys. He was furious and grabbed me, grappling with me to get my keys. He shook me, pushing me against the sink unit, shouting and swearing in my face to return the keys. I was very afraid and screaming for help. He let go, opened the door and flung my cases on to the drive then pushed me outside, locking the door. The driver came and asked if I was alright. I was crying. He took the cases to the car. James came down the drive, and calmly asked for the keys. I repeated I needed them and said he had spares for all the doors, he denied this insisting I return them. Afraid not to do as he said, I took the front door from the key ring and gave it to him. He walked away. I was so humiliated being thrown out of my home in front of the driver, as I left I resolved I couldn't return.

When I reached the airport I phoned my brother and told him what happened. He calmed me down, said to go on with my trip. I'd thought I'd cancel and go home and get my things out of the house. I decided (in order to keep him calm as I needed to get back into the house for my things) I would phone him, which I did and ended up apologising for my behaviour. He said sorry is no good, it's change that needs to happen. I agreed I'd been all over the place it had been a difficult time. He told me he'd written to my daughter to tell her what's been going on (I didn't believe him) and I had to write to him reflecting on things, how was I going to change. He said if this went to court I'd have to undergo a psychiatric assessment.

In transit at Abu Dhabi my handbag was stolen containing my phone, purse, money, cards so I was very upset. Especially about my phone, all my data gone.

My daughter and grandchildren met me at the airport. I was so glad to see them.

It was several days before my daughter raised having received an e-mail from James. I was very surprised. He'd said something about my mental instability, how I'd caused a scene before I left. She hadn't believed it and had no intention of replying. She was very angry about him.

I contacted Davina from Women's Aid. She noted James had got in there first, undermining and discrediting me with my daughter, minimising the incident, it's the fourth time he's been grabbing me. She said getting my keys was about control and to punish and frighten me for going away.

I told her I'd thought of returning for a week or so to try and sort out my belongings and then leave. Davina said it wasn't safe for me to go back. She suggested I contact Women's Rights organisation in Glasgow, and talk to a solicitor there. I did that and over the weeks was given very important advice re: occupancy rights, access to the house, police intervention if needed and definitely not to return alone.

I discussed these issues with my son and brother who agreed to assist me and together came up with a plan. Two lady friends also agreed to help.

…

I returned two days before James expected me, to check with police re: intervention if needed. I was dismayed when they pointed out as I'd talked about domestic abuse they had to take action and interview the perpetrator. I was interviewed later at home by two officers and was given advice about going to the house. They told me James would be interviewed in the next few days.

My return required planning and Davina advised collecting keys, paperwork and clothes first. She warned if James became upset, not to let it deter me. I had friends for safety. My son, brother, and friends met for coffee to discuss how I'd go about this difficult task. I rehearsed what I'd say if he let me in. The guys would remain outside on the road and the ladies come into the house and help me pack my things.

At 1 pm we went up the drive I opened the door, James approached and I greeted him explaining quietly I'd made a decision to leave that day, and said what I'd rehearsed. He looked very shaken, saying I could have given him notice. He wanted to talk about the future, I assured him we would. We began in the study retrieving paperwork, James present repeating he was shocked. I said I couldn't think of a better way to do it. He said we were stripping his house, I said I was only taking my things. He kept trying to engage me and my friends as we packed, I was feeling sorry for him, it was very traumatic.

I advised him the police would be coming to see him, that I had gone for advice only not to press charges. He was taken to the police station the next day, however not enough evidence to charge him. He'd admitted to an argument about keys put his hand on my shoulder to turn me to face him, denying everything else. I felt angry that he'd denied what he had done. Davina thought it would be good for him to hear the accusations - they did happen. These incidents over the years had made my life hell.

...

Several days later, James phoned. He'd had a heart attack. His GP had sent him to hospital for tests and ECG to check his arrhythmia. He said the GP suggested his condition could be affecting his behaviour! He needed to see me, he missed me, his wife. He said his ability to control his anger isn't there. We differ in what happened before I went to Oz. Rejecting him was terrible.

I went to see him. He said he'd made an appointment to see a male therapist. He pleaded he'd do anything, he'd give house, money, etc. to have me home. He raised old resentments. I was there several hours ending up in tears. He tried to hug me, I was distraught and said I didn't want that, to stop it. As I left, he said if we get back together he'd buy me a new car - a red one.

I told Davina I felt guilty about James's ill health, my fault. She said his e-mails are frivolous, minimising and hook me back in. She suggested I make a list of all the demeaning names he'd called me to remind me of the reality of our relationship.

My daughter Lucy was worried I'd return to James and came over from Oz for 10 days which was very kind and thoughtful. She checked his e-mails and he had seen the therapist. She helped me reply, saying we both needed space and time and I'd prefer not to have contact. He ignored my request and replied with pleas to get in touch noting his poor health, tugging at my heart strings. In his erudite 'epistle' he opined we both made stupid errors and quotes forgiveness, redemption and desires to make peace with me.

Despite being unwell, Lucy was a great comfort, helping me deal with paperwork and in decisions for the future. I was feeling overwhelmed, worrying I'd receive divorce papers.

I'd started the list of insults Davina had suggested, crying as I did it, and denial slipping away. It's not the actions of a man who says he cherishes and loves me.

In the next e-mail James pulls out all the stops. Be my wife forever. Admits he's made mistakes but doesn't say what he's sorry for. He proposes renewal of our marriage vows, re-establish relationships with my family and we buy a home together to ensure my married rights. It's full of promise and lovely things. It's very skilled in what he says, bombarding me, no regard for my request for no contact. Davina said the closure I need is so difficult to get because of the heavily invested love I have for him.

Davina told me about Saje Scotland - a project run with lottery funding, for women exploring the dynamics of abusive relationships. I was willing to try anything to help myself. My first introduction was an invite to a monthly get together, for coffee and a chat with other women who'd been affected by perpetrators of abuse. I went along feeling nervous. My anxiety heightened when I saw everyone else was younger than I, some with little children around - I didn't fit in, I wanted to run away from these people, I felt sick - I DIDN'T WANT TO BE AN ABUSED WOMAN - The women were laughing and joking and it grated on me, I couldn't talk. I cried on the drive home. However, I booked a place on the next course.

I attended the first session of the programme with Saje in the middle of April. I found it very difficult and I was surprised that I was crying during it. I wasn't able to contribute and didn't feel part of the group. I didn't want to be like these women. The shame of it. I cried all the way home. I felt so lonely and sad.

The e-mails kept coming. I was anxious if I didn't get one and always upset when I did, feeling like a wimp that I couldn't even deal with an e-mail. I'd forward them to Davina and we'd discuss them when I met her explaining the hooks to get me to engage. Sometimes very cold and business-like, raising a settlement sending me into a blind panic, or flirtatious and declaring his love. I'd started seeing a counsellor who was doing sessions at Women's Aid, I found her very helpful. She said he's trying everything to regain control.

…

I planned to return to Australia for some space and peace, yet was mixed up about it. My son and daughter wanting me far away from James. They were afraid I'd go back to him and I was too.

James appeared at my flat! Angry about people emptying his house. I defended, he'd thrown me out - he mimicked I'd been provocative not handing over his spare keys. Angrily I said why didn't he admit what happened, it was abuse to put hands on someone. He coldly agreed he did, BUT WHAT EVIDENCE DID I HAVE - I said none and he scoffed - well there you are. I was crying by this time. He insisted he loved me - would have died for me, angry re: police coming. We went for coffee, he spoke of my selfish habits, sleeping in the spare room. I was back justifying, unable to stem my tears. He wanted me

187

back as his wife, missed my cooking. I didn't want him to leave, would we meet for coffee or cinema, I said maybe. I felt hopeless, I fear for myself when I want to meet him. He phoned about a trip to Peebles, I fantasised about meeting up, not telling anyone, wanting to go yet knowing I'd be upset. How powerful these desires were.

I started Saje's course, finding some common ground with the other women, identifying with the tactics used. What's OK one day, is not the next. The seduction at the outset recalling James texting, phoning, feeling flattered and special. I saw the isolation as romantic. Psychological and emotional abuse is so confusing, how could I make sense of it. Davina said it's designed to hook you before it unravels you. By that time I've invested so much that I justify it.

I went back to Oz in May and would do the Saje programme again in August. The distance helped clear my head but I was weepy and wavering, worried about James, thinking I'll just go back. In August, James's e-mail entices me with - second honeymoon, a new car, no more 'rent'. It's insulting, emotive. Next he's depressed, he needs me, pleas to honour our vows, an Elvis quote - ' don't be cruel to a heart that's true.'

I start a new course with Saje, I knew I had to keep going. I was relieved when women described their experience of abuse. It wasn't only me, I wasn't crazy, they understood my shame that I didn't leave.

I sent an e-mail to James that he must engage in professional support to address his abuse, his reply was vague. Despite advice I couldn't block his e-mails, I was desperate to know where his head was. His tactics were played out in them, sometimes charming, playful, seductive, others cold, blaming, threatening legal action.

Most nights I'd be reading Lundy Bancroft's book 'Why Does He Do That'. Finding solace in his explanation of 'Trauma bonding' for my emotional dependence on James and why I allowed his gentle massage of my back after his harsh verbal attacks.

Davina assured me it wasn't mean to set a boundary, the e-mails were games, abuse is about control and entitlement. I told her I'd driven past his house going to the dentist.

I joined U3A for people over 50 offering a wide range of activities. I booked for Table tennis, Badminton and Yoga. For an hour I could forget James. I loved it, time for me.

If I didn't hear from James I felt lonely and miserable, and elated when I did - relief he still loves me! Davina said I'd resisted all the promises and now naming the abuse. He'd sucked the life out of me, time to be angry!

In an e-mail I told James that "for me to love him yet be afraid of him was no basis for a relationship" - he replied abuse and physical violence will not be tolerated in our marriage. He wanted an equal relationship not a doormat! He sent details of a psychotherapist for us, recommended by his psychiatrist friend. I agreed.

I was stunned at the cinema by an advert on domestic abuse, featuring the ladies from the Saje project and another weeks later. The film showed a man in a temper swearing, James asked was that abuse, I replied yes.

Therapy started before Christmas. Sarah the therapist raised conflict and James gave a derogatory version of me shouting through his house stripping it. I spoke of the precursor to that before leaving for

Oz, Sarah asked James if he realised that was domestic abuse? He agreed he did. It was a eureka moment, but it was short lived.

We met in a cafe, James looking angry, full of complaints, no warmth from me, no replies to e-mails, his house emptied. I reminded him he'd thrown me out of the house, he said, "YOU DESERVED IT for your behaviour that day". I stood up to leave saying that's a terrible thing to say, then sat down deflated - I didn't leave - James remarked later, "what a passion there is between us".

During the sessions, each 2 hours long, I related the cafe incident. Sarah didn't pick it up. James denied I gave him monthly cheques, dismissed my claims of punishing silences, threats and physical abuse. At the 4th session, she highlighted our polar views, both of us culpable, why would we want to go forward with our marriage so broken. Her remarks had a big impact on me, I was very distressed. I didn't go back. James was very angry.

I did another Saje project - The Toolkit for Life - focus on life skills with both written and interactive work, a lot to get through.

My son and I met with a solicitor to discuss options, legal separation or divorce which I was against. My son suggested I might benefit from counselling during this difficult process. He was right. I wrote to James advising of my intention to separate. I was very upset and shocked by some of his many e-mails, where he was arrogant and blaming.

My last meeting with James was in a hotel. I offered copies of incidents from my journals, he refused them. He blamed my family for our problems, talk of money ended, him saying - you'll get nothing. He reeled me in taking my hand, did I love him, stop the process, I was the woman for him. Let's go to South Africa. We parted at his car. I didn't look back. I had a horrible weekend of weeping. I was beat.

His e-mails keep coming over 150 now, the message is clear – let's meet, we have the ability to make good, so gifted with words.

...

Excitement at the Saje project - a book - to be written by women with experience of Domestic abuse. I started to research through my journals. Once I started writing my story I couldn't stop, memories unlocked and poured out onto copious pages, many more than was required, I was compelled to complete it. I hadn't often referred to my journals, I couldn't remember much of the content. I was shocked at the level of emotional and psychological abuse I'd been subjected to. I berated myself - why didn't I leave - why did I go back - why did I put up with it. I thought it was intermittent, yet my journals tell a very different story - it was happening most days, conditioned to behave in a certain way. A glare, a certain tone, enough for me to comply. I was ashamed when he implied my relationship with my son and family was abnormal, so afraid of his rage.

The book came at the right time for me. I've made a stand. I know my decision to end the marriage is right - ENOUGH now. I'm not willing to accept any more. I tried everything I could, hoping ... HE'D get it... but it was ME who had to get it.

In the midst of all these commitments, the legal business going forward and the Saje book, I was invited to Australia over Christmas and continued my writing amid my tears.

I was at an impasse with the legal process and have had to lodge an action for Divorce.

My son, daughter and their families, have been incredibly supportive throughout. My grandchildren's love is a delight I am so lucky. My brother and his wife have emigrated to Sydney. I miss them terribly. My friends have been so kind and patient listening without judgement and my Woman's Aid worker Davina picked up the pieces so many times, explaining the dynamics of abuse, enabling me to leave and believe I deserved better.

NOW

LOVE?

I was 17 when, as I thought, I met the love of my life. Everything was wonderful, going out dancing or out with friends, often just the two of us and the sex was good or so I thought, lots of nights cuddling in front of the telly being part of a couple felt good. And a sense of belonging. Little did I know that when you're seventeen you don't actually know everything and the world does not revolve around you. But him being a mature 23 year old, I thought that he would know everything and this would be my happyish life for the rest of my days

I've got everything I need just like the fairy tales.

But that was when the fun and wonder stopped; we were married quite quickly. We both worked for a couple of years to build up money. The money automatically went into the joint account. After all, that is what marriage is. As time went on little problems came up like, I didn't suit that colour or you've got terrible taste in clothes, wallpaper, etc. Oh, and your cooking is awful. Slowly started to creep in, but not so fast that you notice the gradual taking away of your self-awareness. If you are lucky the violence has not started yet. Then I fell pregnant and the bullshit started: I was not putting on enough weight and then I was putting on too much. Bear in mind the weight I put on was the weight my baby was born. This was the same with baby number two.

Then the kids arrived.

And all was OK for a while. As the kids got older, I went back to work. At the same time, he became ill. And never worked again. I continued to work twelve hour shifts and was still expected to come

194

in and start to cook, do the house work and all other things "house wife". Like a fool I did it all. I began to resent being the only one doing anything in the house, then on talking to my own mother was told,

You've made your bed so lie in it.

I was confused and hurt that my parents could treat me like this.

He made all the decisions. I did not even get to choose wallpaper or carpets or any of the furniture. I just got dragged along to see what I would be polishing and cleaning next. His drinking became more frequent, larger amounts drinking until he was unconscious. The "blackouts" were more frequent. The only-a-slap became more frequent and harder. I didn't know any different. As far as I knew this was how it was (married life) so from here nothing changed till he decided I was not who he married and was now not good enough for him. I felt so guilty ashamed stupid. How could he not love me. I did everything for him. I took the beatings I took the blame for his actions, I drove him to it coz "I am not right in the head", it was the drink, you made me do it and yet I still worked and handed over the money.

AND I BELIEVED IT ALL.

He finally left and at first I did believe it was my fault. If only I done better - brought more money in, cleaned up better, was just like the women in the porn, didn't push his buttons. He was still trying to control everything. How much I could take out the account, and of course there was the thought, that maybe if I had taken better care of myself he wouldn't have had to look elsewhere. But this was only to keep control of me so he knew exactly where and when I had been.

For the first couple of years I was still stuck in the love/hate relationship then finally pulled myself out of it…

I have my own place, my own car, my own life. I am free to do as I please, the simple things that bring so much joy in my life like being able to leave a cup in the sink overnight, not having to clean things as soon as there is a speck of dust on it.

Now I am SO HAPPY he left. When I see it now I thank the heavens that I got out alive and I smile and thank Saje's group where I have learned that none of it was my fault. That he is the one who has the problems, not me.

I do believe this programme saved me and others who have attended.

My life is now my own and I am living it to the full and loving it.

I will not be so easily ready to jump into a new relationship, with all I have learned…

ANY MAN THAT WANTS TO BE WITH ME WILL HAVE TO BE PRETTY FUCKING AWESOME.

MY STORY

I am not sure about writing this. I hope it helps someone *not to do what I did*. Not to give someone too many chances.

My wolf in sheep's clothing. I met him when I was 35. He was four years younger. Yaas my family ♥ lived together two years including one year engaged. Got married, big wedding. Ten months later along came our son. Six weeks early. I was twelve days in hospital with preeclampsia (OMG I stayed awake for the caesarean)…

Scary and amazing. Our son was beautiful. 5lb 3oz. While in intensive care, we could sleep over one night before taking our son home. My lovely husband wanted SEX. A mother next door was crying, her baby had died. My first stab in the heart. He asked a nurse why Daniel was early. She said it was because I'd had a termination years before. I'd already confided in my husband about it, but that came back from him to haunt me.

Things he said that became normal?

I was in his eyes
A parasite
Retard
Liar
Sow
Lazy
Needy
Crap mother
Slut

Crap taste for house stuff

Cunt

He was better than me

You hate me and will be glad when I'm dead. As if it matters what you think I'll get you back

Threatened to kill me if I left

It was our 3rd argument he threatened he would nail my face to the wall if I just married him for his money and I was thinking of chucking him out... STUPID me tried to prove I loved him and I was nice and honest. Not like his family.

He never liked my friends. Everything that wasn't about him he spoilt. Too many things to mention.

I once asked for love and respect, he laughed and said poor billy. I realised I was dammed if I did or didn't.

He refers to our/ my son as "thingy". How dare he ignore me in my own house.

He thought he was God for about six months and wanted a bust of himself (like in the museum) for his Christmas present. (Where the fuck do I get one!) Also got me to blow up a photo onto canvas, that his amateur photographer friend had taken of him.

He changed one nappy. Took our son on one buggy walk (he said our son fell out of the buggy). Useless twat. He said when our son was four that he was jealous of him. With all this I still tried to make it work. I was so scared it would be a mistake to leave. Didn't trust my own judgment.

I had panic attacks, dizziness, confusion, anxiety, cried too many tears, depression, worthlessness, thoughts of suicide, thought I was going off my head.

He said when our son was about 22 years old that he was my partner. "You are probably sucking him off as well." Vile bastard.

All I have written was from my notes that I kept. So I never went back to him when I left.

We were together 27 years (good times were if he wasn't in a mood).

After a friend's funeral and me sleeping in the spare room for approximately two months, he sneaked through and tried to get in my bed. Then tried to strangle me. My screaming made my son and his girlfriend come downstairs. I had forgotten that they were at home. My son got in between us and I thought they were going to fight. I just picked up the phone and called 999.

Of three charges, he got one guilty verdict. Two not proven. Court was stressful, they made mistakes not getting my son's girlfriend as a witness. Should have been three guilty verdicts. I am nearly four years on since that night I blocked him and every one of his friends. I moved away, my son has his own flat with his girlfriend. We are trying to move on.

Thanks to Women's Aid and their support I am getting stronger. Feeling sick writing this. I made so many excuses for his behaviour. He was bullied by his brother and sister. His mother was a horrible person. I felt sorry for him.

He got six months interdict not to come near the house. Bliss.

2003 I was so overwhelmed and started to write a diary so it left my BRAIN.

He wrote me letters of what he wanted.
1st letter:
Small safe
Money from son's premium bonds
Gold coins
Fossils
Dental tools
Watches
Books and comics
Boots x2

He said we needed to talk about houses and flats URGENT!!

He chucked out a tenant with two kids and moved into a three-bedroom place.

2nd letter
Safe for coins
Dinosaur tooth
Megladon shark tooth (Christmas presents)

And a note: *I would still like to talk with you, even for a few minutes. I am just looking for closure, I have nothing bad to say. You could help me fix things with our son. Hope you are both well.*

He wrote this on the back of a leaflet for "the kitchen of your dreams". In 27 years I never got a new kitchen. He was a joiner. Oh!! Not a carpenter.

3rd letter, 1 year later

I am writing this note in the hope that you will talk with me about this awful situation. I would hope that we could remember that there were years of good times together. There are many practical questions about our properties which would be advantageous to us both to discuss. On a personal note there are things I would want to say regarding what went wrong and why. With all the history we have I would hope that we would be friends. Things were not all bad, most was good. If you would hear what I have to say to you and our son things might not be so bad. This last year has been very difficult for me and I would appreciate a chance to mend some bridges. You could help to put things right with our son and me which would be wonderful as I miss him terribly. Hope you can find it in your heart to talk to me!

To err is human. To forgive is Divine.
Your friend always.

So much happened. I have missed a lot out. But I do know now that I lived with a Convent narcissistic bastard.

My son and I have had zero contact since, and getting on as best we can. It's not been as easy as I thought. Nightmares, flashbacks, etc.

By the way it was my son that told me I was in an abusive relationship.

Got in touch with Woman's Aid and moving on.

P.S.
In the future I hope all men are held accountable.

EXTRACTS FROM MY DIARY

I hate my life when it's like this. I want it to stop

He said it's all my fault. I don't know what to do.

My life seems so shitty, I wish I was someone else!!
Panic attacks are back.

I can't eat. I want to stop feeling scared. I feel so nervous. I can't stand this.

All the rotten things he has said all come flooding back to me. I don't believe he ever loved me. Money is so important to him.

It's terrible living on your nerves. I am lacking in confidence at times. He keeps knocking me down little by little and he can also make me feel great.

He said a few very heart to heart things We talked about our feelings and he admitted he has a problem and if his temper does not get better in one month he will go and see a doctor. I pray he does go to see someone professional.

He was very open about things, said he does not like himself. Does not know why I am still here. I think things are finally going to turn around.

I feel like doom and gloom. I feel very down today. He came home very moody again. Things are not changing. Good one day, bad the next. I can't stand it.

I write things down because it helps me to stop thinking so much. As I am starting to take panic attacks again.

I felt really hurt and down by it all again. I could not tell him this for fear of making things worse.

It was a nice day. All in all a good day.

I am worrying all the time feeling very nervous waiting for the happy bubble to burst. And it does.

Hurtful things were said and I just want it to stop.

I did not handle the situation well. He said he would kill me first if we sell this house.

I feel so depressed. Going to the doctor for antidepressants again. Maybe I have been on them all the time. To live with him and his issues (temper)

I am breaking my heart at the way he treats me. I don't think that's going to change unless we go to marriage counsellor and him to see about anger management.

He called me a liar again. Could not trust me.

Feel like a zombie again

I can't stand it when he talks to me like I'm a complete idiot. I feel totally controlled by him and frightened.

There is too much stress for him and he finds it hard to manage his temper.

We talked. He told me he was jealous, scared of losing me. Thinks I am lovely etc, etc. Apologised for last night.

My head and my heart feels like it's going to burst at times. I hate that feeling. It makes me unhappy. I hope the group therapy will help me be strong and not scared and unsure and negative. I just want to enjoy our life as a family.

I want to note my thoughts today.
I am questioning now do I still love him. Does he really love me. Do we know what it means.

He tells me things like I am everything to him. Which is great. I love him too. Then slowly he moans and picks away at my confidence and I just want him to be happy.

3 things I hate about myself, thinking too much. Smoking. Letting him talk to me like shit. It's not what he says (sometimes) that bothers me. It's the way he says it. When I am dead I think he will miss me. That keeps me going on.

I am fighting the crazy thoughts I am having. I could just top myself.

He started to grab my arm very firmly. Plus pulling at my hair. He was making funny noises. I was really scared. I did not say anything to him.

It's our wedding anniversary tomorrow, I wish I did not feel so sad.

STRENGTH

REFLECTION

"Okay, so you have a couple of options here. You could try marriage guidance, or there is an organisation called Saje Scotland who deliver courses that help women like you who are living with domestic abuse. If you like, I can refer you?"

The psychologist looks at me expectantly.

I have been crying for almost an hour now and I can see she wants an answer so I tell her how mortified I am that we tried marriage guidance before and it ended badly when the counsellor probed a bit too much about my husband's childhood. He gave her a warning that he was starting to get angry and didn't want to talk about it, but she continued and, well let's just say we were asked to leave. And that was our second attempt at marriage guidance so nope, no thanks. Anyway I'm not here about my marriage, I'm here to get help for me.

I am - according to my husband - crazy, clumsy, argumentative, difficult, stupid, riddled with anxiety and dangerously fragile. It is affecting his health now and he feels under a tremendous amount of pressure to hold things together while I fall apart.

She explains that what I have told her in the last hour is actually what is most likely to be causing my anxiety.

Let's be clear here, I am not a complete moron. I knew that my husband had very exacting standards, both at home and at work, but I was really bad at EVERYTHING, from cooking to shopping, answering the phone, to answering the door. You name it – I would fuck it up.

I asked if she could explain about Saje and their work. She did a brief synopsis and I heard myself saying "but my husband doesn't hit me". She simply answered, "he doesn't have to".

I met him when I worked in one of the big pubs in my hometown. He was fun, kind, full of confidence and a very likeable character. A successful businessman, bit of a workaholic and always happy to throw the cash around. He was also married, unhappily, to a crazy woman.

Fast forward three years and I'm a single parent to my daughter who is the centre of my universe. Things didn't work out with her dad but I'm plodding along, getting on the best I can.

He came back into my life by a chance meeting in the street with a friend, who told me he was getting divorced and going through a horrendous time. I reached out and we were soon meeting up with our kids in tow. His girl was a year older than mine. I would often help out and babysit so he took us out for dinner to thank me. And this became a routine.

Eventually we became a couple – not easy with a crazy ex-wife who is calling the police and accusing him of all kinds of violence – he had told me he had been in a bit of trouble in the past because he didn't take shit from anyone and he had this red mist that descended when he was angry or threatened in any way. In most of these cases, the perpetrator will always say his ex is a nut job or crazy. Sadly in my case, his ex actually was crazy, I knew her and she was totally obsessed with attention of any kind and utterly bat shit mental. She hated me and made it really clear.

So around this time, I moved in with him (perhaps not my smartest move in a long list of unsmart moves). My daughter had been ill quite a lot because the house I was renting was damp, old and had no central heating. It was winter. He was so concerned he started getting us to stay at his flat most of the time so, really, moving in kind of just happened.

Within a year we were getting married. I was so excited. I couldn't believe that someone would tell me every day that they loved me so much. There were a couple of little niggles but they were easy to sort out, I just had to watch how I spoke to him sometimes, and he would often say "your mouth is going to get you into trouble, you need to stop being so lippy."

I was known for my sarcasm and quick-witted humour and that had been the basis of our friendship all those years ago, but it seemed now I was losing it a bit and starting to be really offensive. I was careful to watch what I said from then on, especially on a night out as it seemed to set him off if I was being too giggly and having a good time and it's never a nice way to finish a great night, by making him mad at me and ruining his night.

Our wedding day came along and it was fantastic, a brilliant day and all overseen by my husband to be. He liked to have things 'just right' and he was meticulous with things like the seating plan, the hotel, the timing, where we would stand, sit and the ceremony itself, in fact he met the manager quite a lot on the lead up to the big day.

There was a bit of a shadow the week before the wedding when he made a comment to my dad about hitting anyone who chose to hit him first: "man, woman or child – if they hit me first, they are getting hit back twice as hard and they won't get back up". My dad made a point of saying he wouldn't like to think that he would hit me, and was told "absolutely, if she started it". The conversation escalated and suddenly he threatened my dad and tried to get him to fight. It was a horrendous situation and bizarrely, as quickly as it had started, he put a stop to it and became completely calm again.

It was only a few days to my wedding and I was distraught, but I felt I had no choice but to continue with the plans. Anyway, afterwards he was nicer than ever to my parents even though he didn't apologise, but he was being so kind to them and that must have meant he was sorry, surely?

A couple of weeks later we found a lovely new estate in a town a few miles away, a house within a budget we could afford and the chance to put some miles between us and the crazy ex. We bought it. We had been married six months by the time we moved in and as is normal in a new build, there was some extra work to be done such as fixtures and fittings and the outside work of laying new grass, etc. He wanted everything to be done straight away. I'm not kidding. Everything needed to be done within a week. His temper was off the scale and it became a bit of a joke that he was off down to the building site in the estate to see the site manager every morning before he went to work. Things were tense in the house to say the least. I had no car, no relatives nearby and was stuck in a building site nowhere near a bus route. During this settling in period (ironic) he didn't speak to me for three weeks. I pleaded with him to calm down, I begged, I tried arguing, I asked what I could do to make things better for him? I told him he was ruining what was meant to be a new, exciting chapter in our life.

He lost the plot.

He picked me up and ran along the hallway to the bedroom and flung the window open, screaming at me that he was going to throw me out. I was grabbing on to door frames, window ledges, anything to stop the momentum that was going to propel me from the window. He stopped and turned me round and flung me on the bed, but I landed on my head and something clicked in my neck and I was screaming and crying as I slid on to the floor.

I curled up as small as I could and cried. I had no idea what had just happened but I knew I was terrified and in a lot of pain. When I finally got up he was sitting on the bed, calm as you like and he simply said, "what is going on in your head that makes you over react to things?"

That was the first time he didn't hit me.

I couldn't believe it. He went to work as if nothing had happened.

Later that day when I picked my daughter up from school I packed some things and got my dad to come and take us to my parents' home.

I was embarrassed. Of course I watered down the reason I had left, I didn't want mum and dad to worry. He kept phoning though and was talking as though nothing had happened, then he gave me a lecture about how I needed to stop being pathetic and face up to my mental issues and don't let them stop me from having the fantastic life we were about to have.

It is difficult to put into a few pages just how coercive control slowly takes hold, and trust me, I am reading this back and finding it hard to believe I did return again and again but, incredibly, I did. I kept returning. I was completely brainwashed and there were times I would watch him with other people and see just how he had a knack of getting people to do what he wanted them to. He would boast about the fact he always got what he wanted. But confusingly he had a genuinely kind side to him and he always helped people who were vulnerable, so helping old people or someone a bit down on their luck was always something he made a point of doing.

My husband liked to lecture. He loved nothing better than the sound of his own voice and sitting for hours at a time "thrashing out" the current topic that annoyed him (always something I had done) and I wouldn't be allowed to leave the room while he was in full flow. This could and often did go on for hours on end and he was obsessed with me always keeping eye contact with him. If I ever dared to challenge his bully boy tactics he would yet again remind me that before we got married, he had told me all about his temper and that he had been involved in a few run-ins with the police in the past. He had been open and honest and I knew what I was marrying. He even proudly told me that he had said to our best man, the night before the wedding that "the only thing that will cause problems for us is her being too mouthy". He warned me before, he was completely open and still I married him, so this upset was my own fault. I have never felt so alone.

Once these ground rules were set, the isolation really took hold. My friends were picked off one by one, for being too loud, too much of a bad influence, too fake and there were some that I was told didn't really even like me. The thought of a night out was now making me really scared and I would have to make up all kinds of stories to avoid going. One night he couldn't get his cufflink to sit right, apparently I had made a mess of ironing his shirt, I said he was overreacting slightly and that was it, boom! Off he went. I was left nameless, everything was thrown around the room, this was a grown man having a full-on tantrum, he really was a 6 foot 3 toddler. Needless to say, I had to call around and make excuses that I was unwell, all the time I'm trying to keep my voice normal and not give away the fact that I'm crying and scared and tired of picking things up after yet another tantrum.

That was the second time he didn't hit me.

I remember asking him once why he said such horrible, sick things to me when he was in a rage. I tried to explain that adults could argue but even in the very worst of times I never ever wished him dead or said the horrific things that he said to me. He stood over me, got in my face and said, "because if you choose to argue with me I have to destroy you and that means I have to do or say anything it takes to win."

A couple of weeks later, he flipped out one day and picked me up bodily, pinning my arms to my sides and flung me out the front door, down the steps where I bounced off the garage wall, taking a chunk out of my arm and landing backwards, flat out on the grass in the front garden. I always cringe at this memory because I will never forget that the couple next door were bringing their shopping in from the car and they just continued as if I wasn't even there, rolling on the grass, crying and with blood all over my top while he is inside screaming and my dog is going crazy trying to get out to me. That couple never looked at me again.

That was the third time he didn't hit me.

There were many, many more times after this, but I always believed that my husband didn't hit me, because he told me that. Constantly.

After a while, you have handed full control of yourself to this person. I couldn't answer the simplest of questions without consulting a mental checklist to try and figure out what answer he was looking for and would give me the least grief. I fully believed that he didn't hit me and therefore I couldn't call Women's Aid. I hadn't even heard of mental abuse or coercive control.

The mental abuse is a very slow drip feed process, it is the cruellest type of "long con". They will convince you and your family that you are the problem, your behaviour is difficult for them to deal with, etc. etc. Of course, this is all done in a very subtle way, but once they have what I call ammunition on you, it's game on. When you become an item, you are head over heels in love and you tell each other everything about you as a person, the good and the bad. You trust they will act upon that information with respect and therefore be mindful of how each of you would like to be treated. You trust that.

I used to be so envious of women who considered their lives boring. Mine was always drama. Always something that was going wrong, that he had to fix, he was the only person who could fix all these things, whether that was in the business, or for a friend or relative, and the drama always came with the story that we were going to lose this contract or our business or in some cases, our house. He was obsessed with being the hero and pointing out to me and anyone else that I was a liability.

All this was really taking a toll on me. I was anxious beyond all measure with these daily disasters and if I wasn't in the office or house with him he would call me and yell down the phone at how everything was going to shit and I had to stop whatever I was doing and report to him immediately at the office or at home. Eventually of course I believed that everything that went wrong was, one way or another, my fault. He started to comment that I was his bad luck charm, he had always been OK until he met me, why did everything keep going wrong for him? Because of me, of course. The guys who worked for us often saw him humiliate me but he really didn't give a fuck who saw it. They never said anything and I wouldn't have expected them to, they needed their jobs. By this time we had been together almost twenty years.

On top of being a jinx, it turned out I was really really shit at housework, cooking, food shopping and had no clue in the office either. Poor guy was having to bail me out on a daily basis. I could never hit the standards he expected for anything, I couldn't even regularly have his favourite foods in the fridge. He enjoyed nothing more than pointing out that I wasn't coping very well at the moment and would I like him to get me a cleaner? I mean it's not like I had a difficult job, it was a family business and I could come and go all day as I pleased? There are women who would give their right arm to have what I had.

Are you fucking kidding me? Sadly… no.

We would have a really bad spell, his temper would be off the scale and his mind games were exhausting. To give you an idea – I once got a 45 minute lecture about moving the TV 2cm when I did the dusting one day and he couldn't settle in his usual spot on the couch so had to keep getting up to adjust the TV one millimetre at a time, IT HAD TO BE PUT BACK TO ITS ORIGINAL POSITION!

I just couldn't see a way out of this nightmare but I would try to leave anyway, and I would say that maybe we need to split. He would then call my daughter downstairs and the siege situation would begin: we had certain seats to sit on and he was always in between the two of us. He would tell our daughter what mum has done wrong this time and this was followed by a roll of the eyes as he told her, "guess what? Mum wants to leave us AGAIN." This was then followed by the usual, "OK give me the keys to your car, I own that, give me half of this month's mortgage payment and leave everything else too, you came to me with nothing and you will leave

214

the same way, I even own your knickers!" It was difficult not to ask if he found them uncomfortable to wear.

Time after time I gave up. What were the options? Two that I could see... nowt and fuck all.

Eventually he would have a wee spell where he felt sorry for me. We would go to book a holiday. Well, he would make all the decisions but hey I got to sit there and have a tiny bit of input, just enough so that the person booking wouldn't think for a moment that I wasn't a spoilt bitch "who gets everything she wants, don't you sweetheart?"

Every holiday, had a drama. EVERY SINGLE ONE. There were ones where he couldn't eat the food and "he wouldn't feed that shit to his dogs, who the fuck gave this shithole its 5 stars?", he would shout as he walked through the hotel restaurant. There were the ones where he would possibly have to stay up all night to arrange a flight home as "it's all gone tits up back home, I fucking told you I couldn't come away on holiday." There was a real beauty where we had missed a flight - genuinely not our fault, the airline had changed the flight time by half an hour and sent letters out but there were two men on the flight with the same name, one of them got a letter, can you guess which one didn't? I kid you not. Anyway, he went MENTAL at the staff at the desk and security were called to calm him down while the airline staff scrabbled around trying to rearrange another flight for us. This was just a year before 9/11 so he definitely would have been arrested had the same thing happened a year later. Anyway, we got an upgrade, had to do an extra flight and pick up our luggage halfway but we would still arrive at the destination on the same day. I was over the moon to be flying business class. He was not. I spent the first flight trying to calm him down but to no avail. We went to get our luggage between flights, his was there, mine was not. Shit shit shit shit. The second flight we did in silence because it was empty and he chose to sit several rows away from me "too angry to speak". He didn't speak to me for two days. I still find it hard to believe that this behaviour was just another day for me but looking back, there have been so many incidences where I would desperately try to keep the peace or allow myself to be humiliated just because I wanted, just for once, really wanted to be like other couples and actually have a holiday, relax, be nice, enjoy ourselves.

It never happened. I have sat on some of the most beautiful beaches in the world, alone and crying. I have sat in lovely restaurants around the world, alone and crying. Real lonely, deeply sad, silent tears. I would be aware that the people around me were probably embarrassed for me, maybe even a bit annoyed for me or even annoyed at me, he would always make just enough of a scene that he could stand up and walk off in disgust, leaving me sitting there engulfed in shame and fear at the same time. I couldn't even say what they were about most of the time, but they happened with a great deal of regularity on each and every holiday without fail. When my daughter was young it wasn't so bad because we would just go and have fun without him there, but when she grew up and went away on holidays with her friends and it was just me and him, that was really hard. I did a lot of people watching and I became really good at making imaginary lives for other people to keep myself entertained.

When he isn't there, (which wasn't very often in my case), you are so well trained that you will keep up the good work for him. You are so tired and brain washed you spend your day trying to improve on yesterday, trying to get things right, please – just this once for fuck's sake! You have trained yourself to always be on high alert, always looking out for their next move, you pre-empt every scenario in a day but still you will be doing something wrong.

216

Next month will be two years since I ran away from my husband. I did attend the Saje group, he grudgingly gave me two hours off work each week to attend the "confidence class" that I told him I had been referred to (oh how he laughed) and after the initial shock of realising that I was living with domestic abuse, I made the decision to go and see a lawyer.

By week 8 of the programme I had left him.

He never saw it coming believe it or not, but on the one occasion in weeks that I was going to be alone for a couple of hours, I fled. I continue to have counselling to try and process the thoughts and beliefs that are left over from his mind games, and I still berate myself in his voice. I have crippling anxiety which is worse now than it was when I was with him but compared to what I used to call my normal, I'll take this again and again.

I often reflect on how different my life is today. I now have the privilege of volunteering for Saje Scotland, and I do this beside my best bud (who I met on the programme), and each week we speak to women who are going through the same stuff that we did. We tell the women that we know how they feel, we know how daunting it can be, and how difficult it is to realise that the person you loved, CHOSE to abuse you, we listen and we can say hand on heart we have been there. There is a way out, it just takes a bit of help to guide you and in my case, it was the women from Saje who helped me and for that - I will be eternally grateful.

The boundaries set, the rules – ever changing
the house, the furniture, the me, re-arranging
targets never met,
goalposts moved,
my needs never considered or approved.
The insanity we lived in
which you made seem so right
on reflection now, it's all black and white,
but I see everything in colour these days
so vivid and clear, no more in a haze
I think when I try hard, I'm almost the old me,
the me that was happy and funny and free.
You said all your luck was bad because of me
you'd call me your jinx, I'd laugh nervously,
and wonder what more I could possibly do
because I had made changes
Yet you were still you.

ACKNOWLEDGEMENTS

Sally Sinclair

Staff of Saje: Vicki, Stef, Debbie, Laura and Calum

Every woman who shares her story here; you know who you are.

Gwen Gemmell for making our cover look so beautiful.

Every amazing volunteer

Board of Directors

Our funders

Our supporters

All the anonymous friends and family who have supported their loved ones in their journeys towards freedom and safety, in little and big ways.

Gwen Morrison at PublishNation for holding our hand through the process to publication.

The final person who needs to be thanked is Nadia. She got in touch with Saje to volunteer creative writing sessions with women and was convinced to take on the task of producing this book. It has been an enormous piece of work and taken up much of her time. This book would not have happened without her and her kindness. We are eternally grateful.

Thank you all,
Janet Henderson, Saje Scotland

Please share this book far and wide.
Thank you for reading.

FIND HELP

If you recognise yourself or someone you know in the pages of this book, please take the first steps to reach out to receive or offer help. We've put together a list of resources below:

Scotland
Saje Scotland: 01592 786701
Police Emergency: 999
Police can also be contacted on 101
Victim Support Scotland Helpline: 0345 603 9213
Domestic Abuse Helpline: 0800 027 1234 (24 hours)
Rape Crisis Scotland: 08088 01 02 03
LGBT: 0845 027 1234
Shakti Women's Aid: 0131 475 2399
Honour Network Helpline: 0800 5999 247
AMIS Abused Men in Scotland: 0808 800 0024

England and Wales
Victim Support: 08 08 16 89 111
Women's Aid: 0808 2000 247
National Domestic Violence Freephone Hotline: 0808 2000 247 (24 hours)
LGBT Domestic Abuse Help Line: 0300 99 5428
Freedom Programme: www.freedomprogramme.co.uk
Rape Crisis: 0808 802 9999

FOLLOW OUR CAMPAIGN
&
VOICE YOUR STORY

 @herstoryrewritten on Instagram

 @Saje_Scotland on Twitter

#herstoryrewritten

www.SajeScotland.org